D1215662

Haggai
&friends

Sixty-six Perspectives
on Stewardship

Haggai and Friends
Copyright © 2010 by Patrick McLaughlin

All rights reserved. No part of this publication may be reproduced without the prior permission of the author.

Scripture quotations marked (NLT) are taken from the *Holy Bible*, New Living Translation. Copyright © 1996. Used by permission of Tyndale House Publishers, Inc., Wheaton, IL 60189 USA. All rights reserved.

Scripture quotations marked (NIV) are taken from the *Holy Bible,* New International Version®. Copyright © 1973, 1978, 1984 International Bible Society. Used by permission of Zondervan. All rights reserved.

Scripture quotations marked (ESV) are taken from the *Holy Bible,* English Standard Version. Copyright © 2001 by Crossway Bibles, a division of Good News Publishers. All rights reserved.

Scripture quotations marked (The Message) are taken from The Message (MSG). Copyright © 1993, 1994, 1995, 1996, 2000, 2001, 2002 by Eugene H. Peterson. All rights reserved.

Cover Design: Sarah P. Merrill
Cover Photo: Leland Saunders
Leland Saunders Photography
ScriptureExpressions.com
Interior Design: Michelle VanGeest
Cartoon Illustrations: Ron Wheeler

ISBN 0-9788585-2-0

Printed in the United States of America

This book is lovingly dedicated to the women in my life these 57 years on planet Earth.

Jane, you are the very, very best; thanks for going to Sagmont 42 years ago.

Betty Baby, you got all of this started and have been a fan.

Mari, thanks for your godly example to TJ and our children.

Renee and Kristen, you are more than we could have thought or imagined for Seth and Matt.

Miss Abigail Rose, someday you will read this and Gramps will explain the word dedication to you.

Judy, thanks; your labors on this book and TTG stuff all these years have been a mainstay.

Table of Contents

Foreword

As a local church pastor I have always been passionate about creating biblical disciples. That priority continues as I give leadership to a Seminary committed to a revolutionary way to prepare ministers. One of my long-time parishioners and friends has challenged me to take it a step further and be about the task of creating biblical stewards. Stewardship is everything we do after we say we believe and Pat has captured that notion with this study of Haggai. In fact, he has taken it a step further by identifying a stewardship principle in all 66 books of the Bible.

Wise and prudent management of our time, talent, treasure, family, children, investments, relationships, and environment, to name a few, can be daunting. We live in a world that cries out for us to be owners, takers, users, not stewards. As managers in this world driven by money, Pat's message is both theologically sound and timely. The one with the most toys does not win, but the one who is faithful in the small and big stewardship decisions wins in God's economy.

Money is such an emotionally charged issue. Time can be even more valuable than our checkbook and investment accounts. How we invest our God-given talent in His work here on earth is critical to our spiritual maturity. Now, perhaps more than ever, the message of the minor prophet Haggai speaks truth into our lives. "'If you will be obedient servants I will bless you and turn your turbulent times into divine blessings,' so says the Lord God Jehovah." I have preached this minor prophet many times in my thirty-plus years of pastoral ministry. Here is what it has taught me: "Obedient ownership" is the first step in becoming a biblical steward. If we do not honor God with that which He has entrusted to us to manage, He may choose to redistribute it.

The Scriptures are the unfolding story of God's redemption of humanity, but Pat builds a case that they are (all 66 books) a study in stewardship as well. Discover where your treasure is and where your treasure is not as you read a narrative from scripture written some 2,500 years ago. This major lesson from a minor prophet and 65 other perspectives will challenge you to rethink and renew or redo your practice of biblical stewardship. From the foot of the cross to the foot of the throne, every decision you make is one of stewardship. Discover who owns you as you carefully and prayerfully ponder Haggai's message and those of his biblical compatriots.

We want to hear God say, "Well done, good and faithful servant." Part of that commendation is God being able to say, "Well done, good and faithful steward." This book will encourage you in that counter-cultural but Christ-honoring journey.

Dr. Wayne Schmidt
Vice President
Wesley Seminary at Indiana Wesleyan University

Prologue

Stewardship is a term that is often misused and misunderstood. I ask you to consider a new term for stewardship, one that I believe defines the concept very succinctly. If we in the Body of Christ can become "Obedient Owners," we will be well on our way to becoming true Biblical Stewards. "Obedient Ownership" means I manage all God has entrusted to me in a way that honors the owner. All of my time, my talent, my treasure, my family, my relationships, my world, my home, my things, my ministry (all of us as believers are in ministry), my call and vocation, must be wisely and prudently managed according to the will of the owner, Jehovah God our Heavenly Father.

So as you read this book you will see that in many places where I could have used the word steward or stewardship I have inserted "obedient ownership" or "obedient owners." I like to refer to it as O^2. The O^2 part is my DNA code for growing and maturing in my faith where I become an "obedient owner" of these temporary things I own (for a short period of time here on earth) and manage to bring honor and glory to God the Father and to His Son the Lord Jesus Christ. It's all God's stuff and He wants us to own and manage it wisely because it all comes back to Him in the end anyway! You knew that, this is just a quick reminder and an admonition to invest your life in people, hold onto to everything lightly and ask God daily to help you be an "Obedient Owner." I think this will become the new term for stewardship!

Introduction

Growing up in Wichita, Kansas, in the late 50's and 60's, I was instructed by my mother not to discuss three things in polite public dialogue: sex, religion, and politics. Times have changed! Sex, religion, and politics are discussed at will. Now, the taboo in polite public or private dialogue is the new F word: Finances. How much money we make, how we make it, how we manage it, and how we give it are considered a deeply personal matter.

It's time to break the taboo! If we don't start talking soon, we won't have any money to talk about. These are turbulent times. Greedy investors, Ponzi schemes, get rich quick DVDs, variable rate mortgages (VRM), and shady deals are rampant. (VRM should be the acronym for Variable Rate Miracles; it would have taken a miracle for many people to keep up with the rate of increase on those mortgages—and many haven't.)

Pulitzer Prize winning author, humorist, satirist, and longtime Washington Post columnist Art Buchwald, said, "Whether it's the best of times or the worst of times, it's the only times we've got." I wonder if the prophet Haggai, President Obama, and others throughout history would say the same thing, only not with their

tongue in cheek. We cannot live in the past, ignoring inflation; we cannot cash in on the future, bypassing slow-growth investments. We cannot wish ourselves to another point of history when times were better. We have no choice but to live in the moment, in fact, this very moment.

I have lived through a few upturns and downturns in the economy, society, and culture. As I look back, I realize that we have often brought these tough times upon ourselves. Consider this statement from US Senate Banking Chair, Senator Christopher Dodd, as quoted in the November 19, 2008 *Wall Street Journal*:

> *They're seeking treatment for wounds that are largely self-inflicted…. The US auto industry has failed to adapt and we are paying the price.*[1]

Here are just a few headlines that reveal how stewardship is impacting our society, our governments, and our spiritual life and times. Almost all of these are self-inflicted wounds from

"Whether it's the best of times or the worst of times, it's the only times we've got."

how we managed, or perhaps did not manage, our resources.

- "Confidence Hits 16-Year Low" *Tampa Tribune*; 3-26-2008
- "US Was Living on Borrowed Time—Getting Credit Will Be More Difficult in the Future" *Grand Rapids Press*; 10-13-2008
- "US Recession Declared" *St. Petersburg Times*; 12- 2-2008
- "2008 Was A Disaster For Everyone" *USA Today* 1-7-2009
- "Home Sales Hit New Low" *Tampa Tribune*; 1-7-2009
- "German Billionaire Commits Suicide—His Empire in Tatters" *USA Today*, 1-7-2009
- "Budget Cuts May Hit the Elderly" *Tampa Tribune*, 1-7-2009
- "Fed Outlook Darkens on the Economy" *Wall Street Journal*, 1-7-2009
- "Unemployment Climbing into 2010" *Wall Street Journal*, 1-7-2009
- "Corporate Swindler Scolded by Ex-Boss for Unbridled Greed" *The Grand Rapids Press*, 1-7-2009

In a recent movie Alan Arkin's character made this statement when challenged about a lie, "Oh that's a business lie; it's different than a real life lie." We have been living the lie here in America for many years—on "borrowed time," as one headline stated above. Many people have lost their savings, their investments, and even their homes because the lie is finally wearing thin.

The economy is not a Wall Street issue; it is a human issue. We have developed a culture of selfishness: It's all about me! It's the Burger King® philosophy that says you are special and you can "have it your way." We consider our own comfort to be all that matters.

How God wants us to utilize the resources he has entrusted to us doesn't often enter the business deal. It wasn't a consideration for the Jewish remnant in the book of Haggai either, until the economic roof caved in. They went from economic slowdown to economic ruin because of their lack of obedience. Sound familiar?

We Americans and people around the world have absolutely refused to live within a personal budget. I am speaking of our personal finances, our public finances, and, in many instances, even our church finances. We spend money on ourselves like there is no tomorrow and are maxed out on our credit limits, paying late fees, and making minimum payments on bills each month. As a result our capacity to be wise and generous stewards is limited.

A longtime friend and detective once told me that in most murder cases the investigative process is to "follow the money," to find out who had the most to gain from the transaction. My fifty-seven years of life, business, and ministry experience allow me to make this observation: "It's still all about the money!" Our biggest struggle is with our financial resources.

That's why this book is for you. Whether the stock market is up or down; whether you are working overtime, part-time, or have just been laid off; whether your 401 K is millions or meager—the message of this book, and the message given by the prophet Haggai more than 2500 years ago, is a great study in stewardship. The investment of our influence, our affluence, and our time was an important issue in 522 BC; and it is equally important in our 2011 culture.

Follow the money.

Haggai's countercultural ideas impacted, in a significant way, an entire nation; applying his principal of "obedient ownership," a term I will utilize throughout this book—will also have a powerful effect on us today.

These are turbulent times, but we have seen these times before—and by the grace of God we will weather them again.

---

[1] *Wall Street Journal,* November 19, 2008, p. 1, 16.

1

For Sale by Owner:
The Theology of Things

Keep your lives free from the love of money and be content with what you have, because God has said: "Never will I leave you; never will I forsake you." (Heb. 13:5 NIV)

Bold as it is, this statement is one I make with confidence: Stewardship involves every decision we make as Christians, after we say we believe. We have just two questions to ask ourselves regarding "obedient ownership."

The first is, "Are you an owner or a steward?" Disobedient owners hold on to their possessions tightly; stewards attempt to manage the resources that have been entrusted to them. The second question is, "Are you a disciple and a steward?" In our New Millennium culture of "grab all the gusto you can" these are even more difficult questions and issues. Most commentators, pastors, teachers, and evangelists would say our most important task here on earth is to become a true disciple of Jesus. While I totally agree with them, their perspective may be shortsighted. Some will devote their lives to becoming disciples of Christ but will never make the connection between discipleship and stewardship.

"Are you a disciple and a steward?"

Before we examine what a true biblical steward is, let's consider the One whose stuff we are managing.

The Ultimate Owner

What was the first job description shared with us in the Garden of Eden? Wasn't it stewardship? This was God's command to our original parents, Adam and Eve: "I created the world, and all of my creation is perfect, now I want the two of you to manage it."

Then God said, "Let us make human beings in our image, to be like us. They will reign over the fish in the sea, the birds in the sky, the livestock, all the wild animals on the earth, and the small animals that scurry along the ground." So God created human beings in his own image. In the image of God he created them; male and female he created them. (Gen. 1:26-27 NLT)

The ultimate owner did not sell the world to us humans; graciously, he gave it to us to manage. He wanted us to be Obedient Owners!

How did Adam and Eve do in that management/stewardship assignment? Were they able to become masters over all of life and the world, or did they stumble just like we have? (We will get to

Genesis chapter 3 and discuss their performance in more detail later.)

We look around at our affluent country today and can't help but be impressed by the wealth. Prosperity in our western world and in the new global economy is truly astounding—but are people really enjoying this bounty? Remember the headline of a German billionaire so distraught over his crumbling empire he threw himself in front of a train traveling 90 mph? His whole life was centered on his money.

People have lots and lots of money and cool stuff; but unless they are honest with God about effectively stewarding this world God has entrusted to us to manage, their lives will not be fulfilled.

The True Biblical Steward

The deity being worshipped today is the god of materialism and possessions. This worldwide economic meltdown seems to have originated from our personal greed. We sometimes get our "self worth" and our "net worth" confused. We have sold out to this world's system. Perhaps a more honest rendition of the For Sale sign should read "owner for sale" rather than "for sale by owner."

Unfortunately this "theology of things" affects the ability of many people in churches around the world to be disciples, especially here in the West. A disciple is one who knows and follows the commands of his master. He or she is seeking to follow the teaching of Jesus in every possible way. Becoming a disciple is a very important part of the Christian life and walk, but the next step of growth is even more difficult: becoming a true biblical steward.

A steward is one who has oversight of the property and affairs of another—it's a management issue. A true biblical steward is one who provides and administers oversight

> *We sometimes get our "self worth" and our "net worth" confused.*

to his or her world and everything in it. These are people who seek to wisely manage and invest their time, talents, and treasure every moment of every day. The heart is easy to convert; changing a lifestyle is what's difficult.

Many Christians want to follow Jesus with their whole heart, but the obedient ownership issues stand in the way. Show me a steward and I will show you a disciple. Show me a disciple and I am not confident you will always find a steward. Discipleship and stewardship are not always synonymous terms.

Dr. Howard Nourse, my longtime business partner and friend,

has made the statement, "All of life's experiences—from the foot of the cross [salvation] to the foot of the throne [graduation to heaven at death]—are about stewardship." From the very first step in the life of the new believer it becomes a stewardship journey. Whether that journey is five months, five years, or five decades, it is a lifelong expedition.

Show me a steward and I will show you a disciple.

Do you remember Kermit the Frog's famous statement, one that he often put into a melody on television and the big screen? "It's not easy being green." Christians can say a similar thing, "It's not easy being a disciple." And I would add, "It is even more difficult being a steward—an Obedient Owner." While we don't hear it preached or taught much in our churches, the scripture is full of stewardship narratives. The Bible shares real stories of real people struggling with their faith walk, seeking to manage the resources that God had entrusted to them. An Obedient Owner manages according to the will of the owner.

The Stewardship Manual

The prophet Haggai and all of his Old and New Testament colleagues will help us unpack and understand stewardship as a lifetime priority. From Genesis to Revelation there are hundreds of verses on stewardship.

The Old Testament is made up of 39 books; the New Testament has 27. All of those books have verses that deal directly with stewardship. The Holy Writ contains 1,189 chapters and 31,163 verses; more of the verses in the New Testament are on stewardship than love and prayer combined. Both Testaments are a human-interest narrative about life and family and redemption. God has a plan to redeem mankind and help us live as stewards in our world. The New Testament confirms and mirrors the rich heritage and theology of the Old Testament.

How we effectively manage our time, our God-given talents, and our treasure is an important issue in our growth as a disciple and certainly as a steward. Particular emphasis is given on the one area of our stewardship practice we seem to mismanage the most, our treasure.

This book is dedicated to an often unpreached, untaught concept that will help you, me, and others grow in the grace of giving by becoming wise and generous stewards of all God has entrusted to us. If we focus on what God wants us to do as stewards, I believe the greed, lies, and get-rich-quick schemes are going to diminish.

It is with great fear and trembling that I invite you on this journey with me. The fear and trembling is not yours, but mine. It is my sinful nature to be greedy and to hoard my money. I admit it is difficult to live in this world of incredible materialism and not embrace its values. But my lifelong goal has been to be a wise, generous, and appreciative steward of all that God has entrusted to my wife Jane and me. Our goal is to be Obedient Owners and not to sell our heart, soul, and checkbook to this world's system.

Our goal is ... not to sell our heart, soul, and checkbook to this world ....

Please don't be influenced by me, a longtime stewardship officer and fundraising consultant; be influenced in your thoughts and practice by the Word of God, in particular, by the life message and turbulent times surrounding the preaching of the minor prophet named Haggai.

The Book of Haggai

I have always loved the Old Testament prophets. They often had compelling, difficult messages to share. Their message frequently involved repentance or judgment, or both. Can you imagine how popular those guys were with their neighbors and community? The prophets were not loved or appreciated for sharing God's message. In our seeker-targeted, seeker-sensitive, 2011 environment, the Old Testament prophets do not get much "air time" in our preaching and teaching. We still hear an occasional sermon on Daniel or a reference to Ezekiel, but rarely a mention of the lesser or minor prophets.

Ask yourself this question: When is the last time I heard a sermon, or better yet, a series on one of the minor prophets? These are quite rare.

I believe many of the minor prophets get a bum deal. The Timothy Group has served many colleges, universities, and seminaries over the years and their libraries always have a number of books on the Old Testament prophets. I find lots of volumes on the big guys, like Isaiah, Jeremiah, Ezekiel, and Daniel; but the number of volumes always decreases as you get to the minor prophets. Furthermore, I find that even among the minor prophets, none are maligned, left out, or avoided more than Haggai. One seminary library I visited recently had more volumes on Obadiah (the shortest book in the Old Testament) than it did on Haggai. Why is that? Perhaps because Haggai is a tough, difficult, in-your-face, upfront call to biblical stewardship, people aren't readily inclined to read it. However, I would claim that Haggai's message addresses many of the headlines and economic woes we read about and experience today.

Five times this unknown prophet calls Judah to "consider her ways." He was not a bit shy in "shucking it down to the cob," as a dear friend of mine would say. Haggai was straightforward. A fastball right down the middle of the plate, he was bringing the heat. Time and talent are personal issues, but not nearly as personal as treasure (our

We need to manage ourselves and become Obedient Owners.

money). There was no fluff with Haggai, no politically correct statements; it was "absolute truth." The message was clear: "God is not going to bless us personally or as a nation until we rebuild the temple. It's time to make a stewardship decision." We need to manage ourselves and become Obedient Owners.

You

Has there been a time in your life that a close friend challenged you to give careful and prayerful thought to your stewardship practices? Has a friend, a colleague, a spiritual mentor looked you in the eye and said, "You had better get your act together; your priorities are way out of whack! In fact, if you don't reorganize your priorities really quickly, God's wrath and judgment may impact your life." That kind of critique is personal and really hurts. Have any of your friends or perhaps even your pastor asked you, "Are you a disobedient owner or a steward?"

I ask you this: Since you have become a follower of Christ, has every decision you've made been a good stewardship decision? Have you sold out to the economic system, or are you practicing a different type of financial recovery and distribution program? Do you believe that all those things in your personal and professional world are yours? Is your life built around yourself and your possessions, or do you live your life as a wise and generous steward and servant?

Humility is not thinking less of yourself, but thinking about yourself less. If most of your decisions relate to how you can become more comfortable, you're not being an obedient owner. Being preoccupied with how you can acquire more stuff, and giving God a tip here and there, is not being a humble steward. God owns it all;

Your priorities are way out of whack!

your task is to seek to manage the resources he has entrusted to you for God's glory and the betterment of this world.

Being an obedient owner is exactly the message the minor prophet Haggai challenged an entire nation to consider. He challenged all the inhabitants of Jerusalem (Princes, Priests, and the People) to get their priorities in tune with God's. God doesn't need our financial help to make things happen, but I believe he wants our help anyway. God wants us to invest our time, talent, and treasure in seeing his work here on earth accomplished. If we don't make those kinds of investments with God and his work, he may choose to use and bless someone else because they're good stewards.

Practicing biblical stewardship is much harder than it looks or sounds. In its simplest form it's asking first what God wants me to do with that which he has entrusted to me. How can I honor God with this decision? Practicing biblical stewardship is evaluating our use of cars, houses, education, vacation, toys, spending money, 401Ks, and mutual fund stock accounts. It is even about those large and small purchases.

Are you ready to be challenged? Are you ready to be blessed? I believe God's blessings are connected to our priorities as stewards. Will you read this book and begin to graciously challenge others in your centers of influence to take a look at their priorities? Pastors, are you willing to preach and teach on this small but incredible book in the Bible? Are you ready to look at biblical stewardship from God's and Haggai's perspective? If you have the courage…read on.

Practicing biblical stewardship is … harder than it looks or sounds.

Haggai is the backdrop for a lifetime voyage into this exciting area of becoming an obedient owner. We will learn a major lesson from a minor prophet and sixty-five of his biblical compatriots (both Old and New Testament authors). Here is a twenty-first century question for all of us to answer: "Do I own my possessions or do they own me?"

Disobedient Owners beware!

2

It's Mine:
Going Beyond Human Nature

"It isn't what you have in your pocket that
makes you happy, but what you have in your
heart." **Author Unknown**

"Do not conform any longer to the pattern of
this world, but be transformed by the renewing
of your mind. Then you will be able to test and
approve what God's will is—his good, pleasing
and perfect will."
(Rom. 12:2 NIV)

Our youngest son, Matthew, is now a college graduate; he is married, has a real job, and a child of his own. He likely does not remember my experiment many years ago with him and two of his five-year-old buddies. I had been entrusted with the oversight (it was daddy day care) of these three lads for the afternoon, as their moms were shopping. No naps for them—it was all-out playtime! I had been instructed to wear them out so they would sleep well that night.

The three youngsters were playing with Tonka trucks and road graders and the like in our sandbox. (For many years we had a tree house and a sand box in the backyard. We raised two boys and I highly recommend both of those back yard implements for fun and fellowship during those formative years.) We took a quick mid-afternoon juice box and cookie break. After the break I initiated my experiment. I took all of the vehicles out of the sandbox except one green and yellow Tonka truck.

I hid all of the other sandbox toys: road graders, army men, Legos, small shovels, dump trucks, three old spoons. The three boys jumped back into the sand box and I carefully monitored my watch. It took all of seventy seconds for it to happen: Matt had the Tonka truck in a death grip and was yelling to his playmates, John and Mike, "MINE!" *There is only one truck and I have it.* The transition was made from stewardship to disobedient ownership in just one minute and ten seconds. It was not, "Here, it's your turn," or "Hey, let's share." It was the announcement, with all of the body language to go with it, "This Tonka truck belongs to me. It is mine!"

> *"This Tonka truck belongs to me ...."*

It's Mine!

Bad parenting, perhaps, but good research.

If you have children or recall when you were a child yourself, you may recognize that people early in life have a strong concept of ownership. What am I saying? If you are alive, regardless of your age, you know what I'm talking about; we all experience that feeling of "mine." Any five-year-old or fifty-five-year-old often has the same response. It's mine! For the grown man it's not a Tonka truck, but rather a new Toyota truck, and a house on the lake, and a Wall Street investment account. I wasn't picking on Matt by sharing that story; I was telling on myself too.

It is my nature—let me go a step further: it is my *sinful* nature—to be a "disobedient" owner, not a steward. A statement attributed to the great Reformer, Martin Luther, is: "The Christian conversion happens in three steps: head, heart, and pocketbook." Clearly, people in Martin Luther's day had just as hard a time with this issue as we do today. Martin Luther's words, written nearly 500 years ago, are right on target for us today.

It's easy to fall into the trap of disobedient ownership. It is a difficult concept but one you must address as you grow and help others to grow in becoming a steward.

It's Not Mine

Possessing and owning are not synonyms. We have come to accept them as synonymous terms, but it is not so. These earthly possessions (my house on Brooklyn Street, the automobiles, the modular home in Florida, the furniture, the hot tub, the appliances, the children, the dog, the cat, etc.) are not mine, and these things are not yours either. We don't own anything; we merely manage them. Material things are provided for us to

Possessing and owning are not synonyms.

30

use while we are here on earth. I have a Christian Stewardship Association shirt that has this statement printed on the back: "It's all God's stuff and he wants it back in the end."

Scripture tells us that material things have five primary characteristics:

1. They are owned by someone (God).
2. The owner sets the expectations for their use.
3. They are possessed by managers temporarily.
4. How they are used is a primary indicator of the managers' Spiritual maturity.
5. The owner holds the managers accountable.

After thirty years and over fifteen hundred clients with thousands of conversations about assets, I am convinced there are only two perspectives on earthly possessions: You are either a disobedient owner or a steward. Those who are disobedient owners think all of their earthly possessions belong to them. Many erroneously believe they are going to take it with them when they die. Those who think they are stewards/obedient owners understand *The one who dies with the most toys wins.* that all of these earthly goods and comforts have been entrusted to their care and they need to manage those resources according to God's plan and purpose; they are striving to be Obedient Owners.

In those two mutually exclusive lifestyles there is a clash of ideas, beliefs, and practices. The world tells us the one who dies with the most toys wins. God's Word, the Bible, has a different perspective; it does not define people by material wealth, but by character, commitment, faith walk, and heart. As Christians we need to invest in people and opportunities that further the kingdom of God. It is a significant clash of cultures.

I need to be a steward because I am constantly being seduced by covetousness, the worship of money, and the things money will buy. Made by God to use things and love people, I am constantly in danger of loving things and using people. Guess what? You either do one or the other. There is not much back and forth on this one. You either think you own it or you are seeking to manage it.

Of the three things that God gives us to manage—our time, our talents, and our treasure (the three T's)—isn't it interesting that only one has the capability of being controlled and hoarded.

We cannot hoard or save up our time, and we cannot manipulate time; it is a fact of life that time marches on.

A talent, regardless of what that involves, is given to us to be used; use it or lose it, as they say. The best singer or trumpet player in the world must continue to rehearse or he or she will lose their capacity to sing or play like they once were able. Hey, even professional golfers practice a lot. They will hit 300-500 golf balls a day to continue to fine-tune their talent and skill.

Treasure can be, and often is, hoarded.

But treasure can be, and often is, hoarded. We can stockpile it and make the declaration that it is mine. Have you heard someone boast about the money they made and how it was theirs to spend the way they wanted to spend it? Of the three T's, only treasure can be possessed and stockpiled.

Stewardship According to God

Haggai's entire book revolves around the topic of obedient ownership. His prophecy speaks to what happens when our stewardship priorities are in line with God's authority and what happens when they are not. "'The silver is mine and the gold is mine,' declares the LORD Almighty" (Hag. 2:8 NIV).

All sixty-six books of the Bible clearly establish the concept of stewardship, not one of disobedient ownership. It wasn't just the prophets who understood who was the disobedient owner and who was the steward. David, a wealthy monarch, penned the words, "The earth is the LORD's, and everything in it" (Ps. 24:1 NLT).

The apostle Paul challenged the very comfortable church and wealthy Christians in Corinth with a series of questions: "For who makes you different from anyone else? What do you have that you did not receive? And if you did receive it, why do you boast as though you did not?" (1 Cor. 4:7 NIV).

Paul also helped the church in Rome to understand the issue of obedient ownership. In Romans 11:36 it says, "For everything comes from him and exists by his power and is intended for his glory" (NLT).

Stewardship 1611 Style

While stewardship is a biblical concept, it began to further take shape around the time of King James of England. He was responsible for the oversight of the King James translation of the Bible in and around 1611. It was the time of feudal lords overseeing most of what is now the United Kingdom. The concept of stewardship was being fine-tuned and really became a part of the English structure of governance.

While the concept has developed into a fundraising term, it has been and always will be a management term. When we hear the term stewardship in our church or parachurch

A steward then and now is an asset manager.

environment today, often our first instinct is to hold onto our wallets more tightly.

A steward in 1611 and in the year 2011 is an asset manager. The steward/obedient owner is one who determines how the assets can be wisely managed, invested, expanded, increased, and matured. Usually in 1611 it was an English lord who was ruling over an area of about two to three counties. He in turn would employ stewards to help him manage the affairs of a small fiefdom. This asset manager would not pretend that the resources he managed were his, but would act on the best behalf of the English lord that he served. He knew he was not the owner but merely a very concerned and committed manager/steward. If he did not wisely manage those resources, he was fired, imprisoned, or worse.

Imagine a Wall Street trader or commodities broker today being flogged or beheaded in the town square for losing the money he invested for his client. Perhaps we would have fewer "Enrons" and other corporate scandals if stewardship was taught and practiced in our present day.

Stewardship Today

More recent Christian thinkers reiterate the stewardship point in various ways. "It's not about you," Rick Warren states in *The Purpose Driven Life* [2]. It is about God.

C. S. Lewis, the famed British professor, novelist, theologian, and philosopher, chronicled a supposed conversation between two demons in his classic work, *The Screwtape Letters*. In this

> *There would be fewer corporate scandals if stewardship was taught and practiced today.*

fictional, tongue-in-cheek dialogue, the elder demon, Screwtape, reveals to his understudy, Wormwood, the importance of stewardship to the life of the Christian. Screwtape mentors Wormwood on stewardship of the body by addressing chastity, but when I substitute the word charity his teaching describes a life of stewardship.

"The sense of ownership in general is always to be encouraged. The humans are always putting up claims to ownership which sound equally funny in Heaven and in Hell and we must keep them doing so. Much of the modern resistance to [charity] comes from men's belief that they 'own' their bodies...We produce this sense of ownership not only by pride but by confusion. We teach them not to notice the differences that run from 'my boots' through 'my dog', 'my servant,' 'my wife,' 'my father,' 'my master' and 'my country,' to 'my God.' They can be taught to reduce all these senses to that of 'my boots', the 'my' of ownership...And all the time the joke is that the word 'Mine' in its fully possessive sense cannot be uttered by a human being about anything. In the long run either Our Father [Satan] or the Enemy [God] will say 'Mine' of each thing that exists, and specially of each man. They will find out in the end, never fear, to whom their time, their souls, and their bodies really belong—certainly not to them, whatever happens. At present the Enemy [God] says 'Mine' of everything on the pedantic, legalistic ground that He made it: Our Father [Satan] hopes in the end to say 'Mine' of all things on the more realistic and dynamic ground of conquest."[3]

As Lewis so clearly illustrates, the subject of obedient ownership raises perhaps the greatest challenge in our spiritual life and walk: the critical question of ownership. Ultimately we all must ask, "Who owns me? Who is the rightful owner of my time, my talent, and my treasure?"

When Death Do Us Part

I was in Cairo, Egypt recently working with a ministry for a few days, and was able to visit the Sphinx, the pyramids, and the Egyptian historical museum. If this sounds exciting and interesting, just imagine how thrilling it was to actually be a tourist of some of the greatest wonders of the world! Nothing short of awesome.

It is believed that King Tutankhamun ruled from 1334 to 1325 BC. He died as the leader of the recognized cultural center of the world, Egypt. His remains and possessions were well preserved in a crypt in the desert. What I *Who owns me?* found amazing were the earthly possessions buried with him. King Tut had several rooms in his tomb that were full of all kinds of possessions, including two complete chariots to help him make his journey to the afterlife. There was also food, clothing, and lots of gold and silver to purchase things along the way in the life hereafter.

It wasn't only that King Tut was trying to take the stuff with him; those who buried him were also attempting to send it along with their departed monarch.

In 1921 the tomb and all of his possessions were discovered—almost fully intact—by archaeologists; and these objects now sit in a Cairo museum.

Sorry, King Tut, and everyone else who can't bear the thought of leaving worldly possession behind: You can't take it with you and it cannot be sent along with you on the journey.

Here On Earth

You either think you are an owner or you think you are a steward, and those decisions are made while you are living here on earth.

My biological father was a depression baby, born in 1925. He would keep cash here and there hidden around the house. He had been hungry at one point in his life and he wasn't going there again. If the banks failed and his Wal-Mart

You can't take it with you and it can't be sent along.

stock tanked he still had a few bucks for himself and others. My father was frugal to the point of being stingy.

When he passed away in 1999 in his hometown of Joplin, Missouri, my parents had been divorced for twenty-five years and none of us was really very close with Dad. All five of us children flew or drove to Joplin and began to make stewardship decisions in Jack Lee McLaughlin's stead as he had made no future plans. We had no choice but to make stewardship decisions based upon what we wanted to give away, keep for ourselves, throw away, or sell. Those were our four stewardship/management decisions, made on every one of Jack's possessions.

He was not a wealthy man—comfortable certainly, but not wealthy. He passed on without a will or trust agreement. He owned a home on two lots, a truck, a Winnebago, and a chunk of stock—plus seventy-four years of junk. If you have buried a parent you are all too familiar with this story.

In most instances, 45% of an estate is claimed by state and local governments in the absence of a will or trust to guide the settlement of that estate. I know my dad did not always have a kind word and thought for the government. I am confident he did not want 45% of his hard-earned resources to be claimed by the government. Obedient Owners plan for the future of their loved ones by carefully making sure their assets are disposed of in a way that honors their lifelong commitments (often through their favorite charity), God, and their offspring.

I am not sure about my dad's faith. It was a very personal matter to him. The fruit of the Spirit was not always evident in him, but perhaps that could be said about many of us. As I sat in the memorial service I was reminded

He did not want 45% of his estate to be claimed by the government.

of another memorial service many years ago. The individual who passed away insisted this written statement be included on the funeral service program: "Where I am you soon shall be, so prepare yourself to follow me." The custodial staff discovered a bulletin in a pew where grandchildren sat during the service as they cleaned up after the service. A note jotted on the bulletin read, "To be with thee I'm not content, until I know which way you went."

You will most often resolve the "which way you went" issue if a person is living out their Christian life and walks as a true disciple and a biblical steward. Who do you know personally that lives his or her life like an owner, a disobedient owner at that? An even better question is whom do you know who truly practices stewardship as a lifestyle? Is the lifestyle and practice of stewardship one you have an interest in emulating?

Basic Human Questions

Let's be honest about the ownership versus stewardship concept. You cannot be a steward if your priorities do not reflect the Spirit of God in your life, lifestyle, and checkbook. How much is enough? Have we been wise stewards with a little, so perhaps in the future God could trust us with a lot? Is God going to get the attention of our affluent society by bringing us to our economic knees? Are we more concerned about our stock portfolio than we are about our spiritual portfolio? Have we avoided doing what God wants us to do so we can care for our own material desires? These are questions raised throughout time because they are basic human questions.

Can you read this passage of scripture and truly say that you are in total agreement with its perspective of stewardship?

Yours, O Lord, is the greatness, the power, the glory, the victory, and the majesty. Everything in the heavens and on earth is yours, O Lord, and this is your kingdom. We adore you as the one who is over all things. Wealth and honor come from you alone, for you rule over everything. Power and might are in your hand, and at your discretion people are made great and given strength. (1 Chron. 29:11-12 NLT)

Let's get to Haggai and his friends and see how he and they would answer these and many other lifestyle and obedient ownership questions. Just wait until Haggai gets cranked up and preaching about priorities.

---

2 Warren, Richard. *The Purpose-Driven Life: What on Earth Am I Here For?* Grand Rapids, MI: Zondervan, 2002, p. 17.

3 Lewis, C. S., and C. S. Lewis. *The Screwtape Letters: With Screwtape Proposes a Toast.* San Francisco, CA: HarperSanFrancisco, 2001, Letter #21.

3

Haggai:
The Man Behind the Book

*"God's aim in human history is the creation of
an inclusive community of loving persons, with
himself included as its primary sustainer and
most glorious inhabitant."*
— Dallas Willard

*"Of all passions, the passion for the Inner Ring
is most skillful in making a man who is not yet
very bad do very bad things."* — C.S. Lewis

Allow me to hearken back to my seminary days and my biblical hermeneutics class. Hermeneutics and ergonomics are two
terms that seem to fit with a study of Haggai. Getting the book
within the context and framework of scripture to best interpret

what the prophet has written is the hermeneutics part. Ergonomics is a question of fit: where does this little, bitty thirty-eight verse book fit into the Holy Writ that we know as the Bible?

From my perspective, the minor prophets are flat-out ignored. They are short books and often have much to do with judgment. No wonder they don't get much preaching time. Many of us seminarians took an Old Testament survey class at some point and we kind of buzzed quickly through those twelve minor books. We sometimes called it "fan reading." We turned the fan on high, and watched the pages go quickly by.

Unfortunately, we missed some gems of theology, doctrine, and admonition. We missed a number of compelling storylines that would make for a great movie script. How about this for a 522

BC newspaper headline in the *Jerusalem Times*: "Prophet of God Claims Stewardship-Building Campaign will Deliver Nation from Judgment & Wrath." Or how about this: "Stewardship Campaign Helps Judah Bail Out of 14 Years of Economic Down-Turn." Or perhaps, "Haggai Shares a Plan of Correction and Compassion for Disobedient Owners."

The books of Haggai, Zechariah, and Malachi are sometimes ignored and often denigrated because these prophets are thought to have none of the refining fire of other minor prophets like Amos and Obadiah. Instead, their concern was getting the temple rebuilt and speaking pointedly to the Levites. All three prophets spoke specifically to the priests. Haggai spoke to the entire culture of the day by addressing those 3 P's of society: The Priests, The Princes, and The People. Think about it; he addressed the religious leaders, the king, and all of the common folk. Nobody got a pass with Haggai. They all got nailed.

Haggai spoke to Princes, Priests and People

He spoke to a tiny, beat-up, post-exilic community that needed desperately to work together to accomplish a huge task. Their place of worship had been destroyed and

Haggai addressed the 3 P's of society.

Haggai was all about getting them organized (the 3 P's of society) to rebuild it and avoid God's further judgment. Haggai spoke to the mind, heart, soul, and pocketbook of the 522 BC Jerusalem residents, and rallied the troops to rebuild the temple.

Political Opportunist?

A short history lesson would be helpful here so you can put things in perspective.

Darius I Hystaspes, in whose second year Haggai ministered (1:1), came to the throne of the Persian empire in confusing circumstances. His predecessor, Cambyses, returned through Palestine from an Egyptian campaign, learned of a serious rebellion at home, and died somewhat mysteriously. (Poison is likely.) His relative, Darius, supported by the army, returned to Media and overthrew the rebellion. It took Darius two years to restore calm to the empire. Jerusalem was in the large satrap of "Babylon and Babylon beyond the River" with one superintendent governor and district governors in Jerusalem and Samaria.

By 520 BC, Darius had absolute control of the Babylonian empire.[4] Haggai was not a political opportunist seizing on the empire's difficulties and using this brief moment of peace to launch a capital campaign (rebuilding the temple). He did not use this as a cloak for the national ambitions of fifty thousand Jews who had returned from captivity over the past sixteen years. No, Haggai was true to his prophetic calling and theology. He was simply being a mouthpiece for God, calling people back to Jehovah and challenging them to leave their economic, spiritual, and political future in his hands.

Sixteen years prior to Haggai's preaching, no one needed to hear the message of stewardship. The Israelite people were thrilled to be doing God's work! They had been miraculously released to pursue the national dream, and they undertook it with vigor.

> *Haggai was a mouthpiece for God.*

In 538 BC the Persian emperor Cyrus made a decree allowing the exiles led by Zerubbabel to return to the land of Judah.

> *This is what King Cyrus of Persia says: "The LORD, the God of heaven, has given me all the kingdoms of the earth. He has appointed me to build him a Temple at Jerusalem, which is in Judah. Any of you who are his people may go to Jerusalem in Judah to rebuild this Temple of the Lord, the God of Israel, who lives in Jerusalem. And may your God be with you!* (Ezra 1:2-3 NLT)

The Babylonian leader was used by God to challenge the nation of Judah to rebuild. The people began the journey back to their homeland immediately after the decree. At the site of Solomon's temple they built a small altar and reinstituted the sacrifices called for by the Mosaic law (Ezra 3). The work on the temple began almost immediately with the foundation being laid amidst the shouting of the young men and the tears of the old (Ezra 3:10-13).

> *Many of the older priests, Levites, and other leaders who had seen the first Temple wept aloud when they saw the new Temple's foundation. The others, however, were shouting for joy. The joyful*

shouting and weeping mingled together in a loud noise that could be heard far in the distance. (Ezra 3:12-13 NLT)

In the sixteen years that followed (as we will see from the text and the next chapters) the people built houses, tried to restore their fields, and went about their daily tasks; but no more work was done on the Lord's house until the prophets Haggai and Zechariah rebuked and challenged the people (Ezra 4:24-5:2).

The people originally had high and lofty plans to rebuild the temple, but upon their return from Babylon they found the land impoverished by the exile. The original zeal of the people to rebuild the temple grew cold. Two years in and, without much progress, the work on rebuilding the temple of the Lord ceased altogether because the Samaritans in neighboring countries began to interfere and throw up roadblocks.

The work did not start again for fourteen years.[5]

The task of rebuilding the temple—the reason many had returned—was suddenly arrested by the scheming of their enemies. Discouragement and suspicion began to creep into their hearts. Skepticism, materialism, and worldliness soon became the prominent traits of their character back home in Jerusalem. Having no heart for the work of God, the people turned to the greedy advancement of their own private affairs.

> *Discouragement and suspicion began to creep into their hearts.*

Does that sound at all like the church in the twenty-first century?

In the second year of Darius' reign, he reaffirmed Cyrus' edict authorizing the Jews to rebuild their temple.[6]

It was evident they needed a point person, a campaign director, a prophetic voice to reenergize the temple project. They needed a man with the guts, gumption, and, most of all, the clear hand of God upon his life so the people would take note and listen. Finding such a man would not be easy. Just imagine if you shut down a building project today and did not touch it for fourteen years. What would it take to get it going again? Political pressure, a massive downturn in the economy, a "Holy Discontent" of biblical proportion? Perhaps it includes all of the aforementioned circumstances.

Who but God knew that waiting in the wings was a man ready to be used as a change agent? This man was so confident of God's message that he risked his life, his reputation, his all. His name was Haggai.

A holy discontent of biblical proportions.

Crazy?

I have often wondered what qualities it took to become a prophet of God in Old Testament times. Did Haggai feel called or crazy? I suppose they are the same qualities it takes to be a prophet today. Whether Haggai felt called or crazy, he was a man of great conviction.

There is a country music tune, "That's My Story and I'm Sticking to It." Haggai appears to be saying, "That's God's story and I'm sticking with it!" A prophet spoke the truth and was always right because his message was from God.

I have been a baseball umpire for over twenty years. Umpires have an adage, "I might not be right, but I have never been wrong." It is not true, of course, but you get the idea. All good umpires are men and woman of conviction. You have to make the right call regardless of how unpopular it may be. Over the years I have made a number of calls that have impacted the outcome of a game. Trust me, whether behind the plate or on the bases, as an umpire I have made my share of bad calls. Yes, here I am admitting it: I have been wrong on a call or two (or 632) over my career as an umpire.

A prophet must speak the truth no matter how unpopular it is with the leaders and the people. A prophet knew he or she could speak with conviction because the message came from God and was one hundred percent correct. Haggai was just such a person to share this great convicting message to Judah.

Mystery Man?

There is not a lot of background information on Haggai, but here are some facts we know about the man. He was a prophet of the Lord. While his ministry and prophetic message was short—his recorded public ministry occupied fifteen weeks during the year 520 BC—he was the most fixed of any prophet; he had a one-track mind and it was on track. Repent of your sins of apathy, rebuild the temple, and God will once again begin to bless you. That was the message, his only message. Short, sweet, and to the point.

Theologically Haggai was thoroughly orthodox, though he alluded only once to the covenant in the second chapter (2:5) where he names many of the leaders in the Davidic line that returned from captivity in Babylon. It is estimated that around 42,360 people returned from captivity.

He is mentioned outside the book only in Ezra 5:1 and 6:14. There he is referenced along with Zechariah as the prophets primarily responsible for prompting the people of Judah to rebuild the temple in Jerusalem and gain prosperity.

At that time the prophets Haggai and Zechariah son of Iddo prophesied to the Jews in Judah and Jerusalem. They prophesied in the name of the God of Israel who was over them. (Ezra 5:1 NLT)

So the Jewish leaders continued their work, and they were greatly encouraged by the preaching of the prophets Haggai and Zechariah son of Iddo. The temple was finally finished as had been commanded by the God of Israel and decreed by Cyrus, Darius and Artaxerxes the king of Persia. (Ezra 6:14 NLT)

It is difficult to catch Haggai's lines of family background, age, character, and other personal details. In both of the previous passages Zechariah is listed as the son of Iddo; hence his family linage is very easy to trace. Not so with Haggai; no mention is made of his family anywhere in scripture, Jewish history, or folklore. Haggai so identifies himself with rebuilding the temple and reestablishing Davidic authority that his own personality is hidden from the reader. Unlike pre-exilic prophets, whose sole authority was the conviction of their conscience, Haggai was not forced to reveal too many tensions of his private life. In this respect he differs especially from such prophets as Hosea (who married a prostitute) and Jeremiah (who wept often for the sinful ways of Israel and called for their destruction).[7]

Each time he is mentioned in Ezra, Haggai (along with Zechariah) is urging for the rebuilding of the temple. They both had a similar call on their life: to make sure the temple David initiated and Solomon built got rebuilt. Yet the separate books of Haggai and Zechariah never link the two men together. Why? Was there some personality clash, or jealousy, or envy, or whatever? Was this Democrat vs. Republican, Sunni vs. Shiite? It seems very unlikely that in a small place like Jerusalem there were two gents who did not know each other. Perhaps they were both speakers at a post-exilic conference or shared their thoughts on the speaking tour by being joint presenters of the seminar "Temple Rebuilding 101." Even without the Internet and cell phones, surely word of mouth would have caused them to meet.

Zechariah preached for a longer period of time and, to that extent, eclipsed Haggai; so often he gets top billing over Haggai, even though

Zechariah gets top billing over Haggai.

Zechariah's message was not as compelling. It doesn't seem right:

50

the guy with the tough message who really impacted the nation with his prophecy gets displaced.

Haggai brought both bad and good news to the people. The bad news was, "God is judging you for your lack of faith and lack of work on rebuilding the temple" (Hag. 1:4-6). He closes out his prophecy

> *Haggai brought both bad and good news.*

with good news: God is so pleased he is going to "bless you" and show you off as His own "signet ring" (Hag. 2:14-26).

We know virtually nothing about Haggai except what his book and Ezra report. He was a prophet of God; his recorded and very short public ministry in 520 BC was a catalyst that led to the building of the second temple. Anything beyond this brief mention in scripture is legend or hypothesis, equally profitless. We can, however, read between the lines for more information.

Haggai left for us only what we needed to know about his life and personal walk with God. He enjoyed the highest honor known to mankind: he was the Lord's Prophet (Hag. 1:1), God's messenger with Jehovah's commission (Hag. 1:13).[8]

Haggai's name means "my feast" or "festival," perhaps indicating he may have been born during a Jewish holiday. The Feast of the Tabernacle was often referred to as merely "The Feast." Was he a shepherd, or was he a farmer? Both are good possibilities, but there is nothing conclusive. Was Haggai an older man? Was he a young boy who was among those who hid and were never deported to Babylon in 587 BC? If so, then for sixty-seven years prior to his prophecy he would have lived in and around Jerusalem. This seems to be a good possibility because the other prophets who were part of the 522 BC exile (like Zechariah) have a genealogy.

All that I can conclusively share with you regarding Haggai is that he knew well the conditions of the land around 520 BC and he spoke with conviction about them. He was a man willing to be used of God in bringing a nation to its knees and back to prominence in Judah and throughout the Middle East.

A Major Lesson from a Minor Prophet

Haggai prophesied in Jerusalem, a city that lay in ruins, without the protection of walls. The temple was in ruins and was hardly appropriate for worship and sacrifice. The whole region was experiencing a major league drought (Hag. 1:9-11). The city, which at one time had more than a hundred thousand inhabitants, now numbered no more than thirty thousand.

Essentially the book is presented in four sermons. The first is placed "in the second year of King Darius, on the first day of the sixth month" (Hag. 1:1 NIV), which would be August 29, 520 BC. The final sermon was shared "on the twenty-fourth day of the ninth month" (Hag. 2:10 NIV), around December 18, 520 BC.

The sermons could be simply defined in this manner:

Criticism Of The People	Haggai 1:1-5–2:10-14
Their Miserable Condition	Haggai 1:6-11–2:15-17
Return To Grace	Haggai 1:12-14–2:18-19
Messianic Oracle	Haggai 2:2-9–2:20-23 [9]

After his prophecy was completed and the temple rebuilt, he did what most of the prophets did; he disappeared. The events in this

Haggai is presented in 4 sermons.

book covered a short four-month period in the life of Judah, but had a profound impact on the entire region. Haggai's mission, vision, and core values in the book were simple: first, to rebuild the temple as a central place of worship for Judah; second, and fairly close behind, to restore the line of Davidic rule.[10]

His message is going to remind the children of Israel/Judah that they are stewards, not owners. He reminds them they have been chosen, and must continue to implement God's demands for a blood sacrifice, an atonement for their sins—obviously a precursor to the sacrifice Jesus will make five hundred years later to deliver his people from their sins. Israel will reject God's plan for their salvation and not acknowledge that Jesus is their Messiah.

This book has a strong Messianic theme, as so many Old Testament books do. The Trinitarian God of the Old Testament is clearly revealed in his Son Jesus and the sending of the Holy Spirit in the New Testament. Here is another example of an Old Testament book pointing Israel, and later us Gentiles, toward the perfect sacrifice, the bloodshed on the cross for the sins of the world.

His book is one of correction and comfort. To me personally it is a book of obedience. As Samuel says to King Saul, "What is more pleasing to the LORD: your burnt offerings and sacrifices or your obedience to his voice? Listen! Obedience is better than sacrifice" (1 Sam. 15:22 NLT). As it was one hundred years later with Haggai and the Judean exiles, so it is today. God won't force us to be stewards and disciples, although we know that is his desire for our lives. He wants us to obey his Word (both Old and New Testaments) and live our life under his authority.

Haggai's book is one of correction and comfort.

In a more universal context, Haggai speaks to what should be our life-long journey to become Obedient Owners. When we don't obey his Word or his commands, God speaks to us personally about a course of correction. Once that correction is made, he once again comforts us and reminds us of his promises.

That is what this concise book is all about. It's a call to people who had lost their first love for God and had taken a course of apathy and disobedience. God slapped them upside the head as a nation and said, "Do my work! Be obedient by finishing the temple and I will bless you." Haggai is a very brief book about

A call to people who had lost their first love.

a nation falling away. God loved them so much that he disciplined them and then showed once again his great love for Judah.

God continues to ask the question today: "Why won't you trust me, when all I have ever done is clearly display my great love for you personally and as a nation?" I won't try to tempt you into thinking further about a current relevance of this book; I will save that for subsequent chapters. (Here's a hint: red, white, and blue.) For now, let's go verse by verse and see if we can continue to glean some additional wisdom from God's Word on how to conduct our lives as stewards, as Obedient Owners.

---

[4] McComiskey, Thomas Edward. *The Minor Prophets: An Exegetical and Expository Commentary.* Grand Rapids, MI: Baker Book House, 1992, p. 966.

[5] Moore, T. V. *A Commentary on Haggai, Zechariah and Malachi.* A Geneva series commentary. London: Banner of Truth Trust, 1979, p. 49.

[6] Moore, p. 50.

[7] Stuhlmueller, Carroll. *Rebuilding with Hope: A Commentary on the Books of Haggai and Zechariah.* International theological commentary. Grand Rapids, MI: W.B. Eerdmans, 1988, p. 11.

[8] McComiskey, p. 964.

[9] Stuhlmueller, p. 15.

[10] Stuhlmueller, p. 16.

4
Rebuild:
For the Love of God

"Treat people as if they were what they ought to be, and you help them become what they are capable of becoming." — Goethe

"A vision we give to others of who and what they could become has power when it echoes with what the Spirit has already spoken into their souls." — Larry Crabb

We think our world in 2011 is complex, but that was before we heard about ancient Israel. Now think about it, here is an entire nation of defeated, downtrodden, former slaves who finally get to go home. But to what? Your former tyrannical, Babylonian master releases you to go home with one simple agenda: "Rebuild the temple."

Ironically, it was the Babylonians that had destroyed the temple in the first place. Perhaps as a way to make up for their previous behavior they were now saying, "Hey, we're sorry for messing with Judah, the people of Jehovah, so we are trying to make it right."

So the Babylonians, their slave master of about sixty years, sent them back home to rebuild the temple and restore the land. That's pretty simple and straightforward, right? Well, not exactly. They went back home, got a good start on the temple and the walls around Jerusalem, and then it stopped; it all came to a screeching halt. There was a bit of pushback by their neighbors, and so they threw up their hands and quit. It was the old, "If you can't fight and you can't flee, then flow." Was it a slave mentality they brought back from Babylon? No one knows the real reason, but the work that had just begun came to a dead stop. This delay in the rebuilding of the temple would last for fourteen long years.

How interesting that the two dominant influences in the lives of these exiled Jews, the Lord God Jehovah and Cyrus (the reigning Babylonia monarch), both wanted the temple rebuilt and restored. God used the Babylonians, the Hittites, the Jebusites, and many other "ites" to accomplish his divine will. Throughout scripture, God uses his people and those non-believing, pagan nations living around his people for his purposes. I believe it was the perfect will of Jehovah that they restore the temple at this time in a timely fashion.

Just Do It

Obedience in a timely fashion was not just a chink in the armor of the people of Judah, it is a human trait we all share. Procrastination is not one of the seven deadly sins mentioned in the

Holy Writ, but it often prevents us from being obedient to God's commands and directives in our lives.

Rolling the clock forward three thousand years, timely obedience is something we all struggle with as disciples and stewards. "Often our struggle as Christians is not in deciding whether we should obey Christ, but in obeying immediately. We may acknowledge our need to follow Christ and commit ourselves to do what He has told us. Yet when God reveals His will to us, that is the time to obey! God's revelation of His will is His invitation to all of us to respond immediately."[11]

Sometimes when I study the scripture and read narratives of the children of Israel and Judah, I think, "Why are you being so stubborn, so disobedient, so stupid?" Then I compare it to my own life and know that I too have been all three of those and more. At times I have put off an immediate command for my own willful pleasure. At times I have been an unwise steward and have no doubt

Why so stubborn, so disobedient, so stupid?

misused what God has entrusted to me to manage. Perhaps you've never been there, but unfortunately I have a time or two or two hundred.

Thankfully God is gracious, as we are going to see in Haggai. But first, another thought from the New Testament.

Some would-be disciples (and obedient owners) pledged their willingness to follow Jesus, but they told him they were not ready yet. Consider the parallel passages in Matthew 8 (vss. 21-23) and Luke 9 (vss. 59-61). This man had an opportunity to walk with the Son of God, yet the concerns of life were competing for priority with obedience to God. He seemed to be willing to follow Jesus, but he wanted to wait until he could bury his father before going along with Jesus. In that day, a Jewish man was responsible to make sure his parents received a dignified burial, so this would seemingly have been an honorable reason for a short delay—a good bit less of a delay than the fourteen-years mentioned in Haggai. The man had to choose between his earthly responsibility and heeding the call from the Lord. The message was clear. Not even the briefest of family responsibilities should impede one's immediate call to obedience.

> *Invitations from God sometimes come with a limited opportunity to respond.*

Timing our obedience is crucial. Invitations from God come with a limited opportunity to respond. Some opportunities to serve him, if not accepted immediately, will be lost. (Fortunately, the temple rebuilding team is going to get another chance.) Occasions to minister to others may pass us by. When God invites us to intercede for someone—or

to step out in faith or to build or rebuild—it may be critical that we stop what we are doing and immediately adjust our lives to what God is doing. Missing opportunities to serve the Lord can be tragic; it can impact our money, or our livelihood, our safety, our faith walk, or all of the above—as we will soon see from Haggai, chapter one. "When an invitation comes from God, the time to respond is now."[12]

Let's look at a compelling message Haggai delivered to the people to help them get their act together and get back to work on rebuilding the temple. This message is delivered in chapter 1, verses 1 through 15a.

The Best of Times

After 14 years of delay, here are the words of Haggai written to the Jewish exiles in Jerusalem:

On August 29 of the second year of King Darius's reign, the LORD gave a message through the prophet Haggai to Zerubbabel son of Shealtiel, governor of Judah, and to Jeshua son of Jehozadak, the high priest.

"This is what the LORD of Heaven's Armies says: The people are saying, 'The time has not yet come to rebuild the house of the LORD.'"

Then the LORD sent this message through the prophet Haggai: "Why are you living in luxurious houses while my house lies in ruins? This is what the LORD of Heaven's Armies says: Look at what's happening to you! You have planted much but harvest little. You eat but are not satisfied. You drink but are still thirsty. You put on clothes but cannot keep warm. Your wages disappear as though you were putting them in pockets filled with holes!

"This is what the LORD *of Heaven's Armies says: Look at what's happening to you!"* (Hag. 1:1-7 NLT)

Haggai encourages the people to begin the task of rebuilding the temple. Remember they had discontinued the project fourteen years earlier. I am confident they had their reasons and excuses down to a science. "Times are hard. The economy really stinks. We have terrible neighbors who continue to threaten us! We are poor and we're slaves just back from sixty years of captivity. Our crops will not grow because of early global warming/drought. Come on, Haggai, cut us a break, things have not gone very well since we have been back from Babylon!"

Times are hard and the economy stinks.

Haggai's message to the people was very clear: "Yes, times are bad and you have no one to blame but yourselves. If you will simply obey God and rebuild his house—the temple—judgment will turn into blessing."

Haggai was a prophet with one message. He represented the God whom he loved to call the LORD Almighty, the LORD of hosts. The God of Israel and Judah was the source of all power, the controller of armies, on earth and in heaven. It followed that his Word had authority; the weather obeyed his commands; the whole universe was in his grasp and would one day be shaken by his hand. This same God was consistent in his dealings with men. Though the Israelites disregarded him (for at least fourteen years), he never gave up on them. When they failed to fulfill his will, he made life hard for them so that they would seek him (Hag. 1:5). Haggai listed no catalogue of gross sins, just disobedience and a lackadaisical attitude that we see so prevalent in the church today.

The Jews who returned to Jerusalem appeared to have been

law-abiding at this time, restrained still by continuing memories of the exile. What was lacking was dissatisfaction with things as they were, and

Judgment will turn into blessing.

the consequent drive to initiate action. Resignation killed faith. The ruined skeleton of the temple was like a dead body decaying in Jerusalem. How could the offence be removed? By a concerted effort to rebuild—this would be proof and pledge of a change of attitude from resignation to faith. God must have asked over those fourteen years, "Is anyone out there listening to me? Who among you will heed my Word in simple obedience and pick up some broken stones, mix some mortar, and begin to restore the temple?"

Haggai's message was simple, "If you get your priorities right, the Lord will bless you." It's clear to me, as it was to Haggai, that these people of Judah just flat out did not want to be stewards. They did not want to rebuild the temple. They did not like what was going on around them, but they just wanted all of it to go away. Perhaps an organizational statement of theirs was, "Whether it's the best of times or the worst of times…it's the only time we've got. Let's just suck it up and keep a stiff upper lip and persevere. If we hang tough maybe things will somehow get better."

No Time Like the Present

Notice in verse one, Haggai's message is marked with a date, something that did not always happen in Old Testament prophecy. We will look at the significance of that time line a bit further in our study. Haggai's message is to everyone in verse (1:1)—to the Princes (the Monarch), the Priests (the Levites), and the People. He is basically saying, "Hey gang, we have been dinking around with this project for almost all of the sixteen years we have been back from Babylon. Isn't it about time we got it built? And, oh, by the way everyone—yes, all of society—is equally guilty and responsible for this lack of action. Hence nothing in your current culture is really working—no food, no clothing, no money, but most of all no true fellowship with God. No one is fulfilled, satisfied or happy. The tough answer is crystal clear, and your lack of obedience has finally caught up with you. You have refused to be wise and generous stewards so I will judge your society and everything around you harshly."

He asks them why they were living in luxurious homes (the Hebrew word might be best translated as paneled or finished houses) while God's house was lying in ruin (Hag. 1:9). Good question! For fourteen years, since they quit building, they have given no answer; so God speaks to them through the economy, their businesses, their agriculture, their own bodies. "Things are not going to go very well until you rebuild the temple. You don't have to do it but you will continue to suffer the consequences."

You have refused to be wise and generous.

Five times in this short prophecy, Haggai asks the people to "consider their ways." Each time he cranks it down a bit more as he asks, "Consider how things are going for you. If you don't like your lot in life, that can change if you will just obey." Every time the question came up before, the people replied in unison, "The time has not yet come to rebuild the house of the LORD" (Hag. 1:2). They gave their collective answer, and Haggai gave them God's response. "Rebuild and rebuild now. You only thought you had it tough before."

I wonder how this initial message and the questioning of existing priorities would play in our churches today. My guess is that it would not go over very well; we don't want the message to get too up front in our faith walks. We don't always like the tough questions; we'd prefer affirmation of what we do right and enabling to continue what we shouldn't. Commitment and obedience have a high cost in our 2011 church culture—just as they did in Haggai's day. I can't imagine they were overjoyed to hear such a difficult challenge.

The Grapes of Wrath

You thought the first part of chapter one was tough? Compared to what came next, that was fire-and-brimstone lite.

Now go up into the hills, bring down timber, and rebuild my house. Then I will take pleasure in it and be honored, says the LORD. You hoped for rich harvests, but they were poor. And when you brought your harvest home, I blew it away. Why? Because my house lies in ruins, says the LORD of Heaven's Armies, while all of you are busy building your own fine houses. It's because of you that the heavens withhold the dew and the earth produces no crops. I have called for a drought on your fields and hills—a drought to wither the grain and grapes and olive trees and all your other crops, a drought to starve you and your livestock and to ruin everything you have worked so hard to get. (Hag. 1:8-11 NLT)

Ouch! I think Jehovah is a bit angry. He forewarns the people about the wrath he plans to exact on the land, the cattle, and ultimately the people. They are working hard, and have been since they got home from Babylon. It seems they just can't catch a break. God lets them know he has observed their stinginess, their self-centeredness, their proud sense of self preservation. His wrath and judgment is an economic one. He will match their lack of obedience with a drought that dries up the fields and hills; the grapes wither, the vegetables die off, every living creature is hungry. They were not tithing, they were not giving—and all of their hard work on their own projects and property was blown away.

Ouch! I think Jehovah is a bit angry.

Is God displeased with us? Is our up and down economy part of his wrath? Have we been faithful stewards? I wonder how many people who found themselves upside down with variable rate mortgages could somehow relate to this passage of scripture. Becoming an Obedient Owner is not any easier a concept to follow today than it was 2,500 years ago. God obviously still brings judgment and consequences upon individuals, their talents and treasure, just as he did for those Jewish exiles. Jehovah got their attention and he may get our attention as well. Are we experiencing God's wrath?

Haggai is telling the people of Judah the solution to the past and present economic depression: Build God's house! Why rebuild? It seems clear from verse 8: So that Jehovah may take pleasure in it and that *he* might be honored.

Could it be that Judah, by ignoring the work of building the temple, was disrespecting God? He wanted to be honored, and they were dissing him! Could it be in our 2011 culture that we too have been dissing God and, in fact, continue to do so? Their day of reckoning had arrived; I am afraid ours is yet to come.

Now let's see the path the people of Judah took once they decided to listen to God and how his wrath turns about.

Can You Hear Me Now?

The people of Judah were finally ready to listen to Jehovah's message passed along through Haggai.

Then Zerubbabel son of Shealtiel, and Jeshua son of Jehozadak, the high priest, and the whole remnant of God's people began to obey the message from the Lord their God. When they heard the words of the prophet Haggai, whom the Lord their God had sent, the people feared the Lord. Then Haggai, the Lord's messenger, gave the people this message from the Lord: "I am with you, says the Lord!"

So the Lord sparked the enthusiasm of Zerubbabel son of Shealtiel, governor of Judah, and the enthusiasm of Jeshua son of Jehozadak, the high priest, and the enthusiasm of the whole rem-nant of God's people. They began to work on the house of their God, the Lord of Heaven's Armies, on September 21 of the second year of King Darius's reign. (Hag. 1:12-15 NLT)

Is it really that difficult to listen to God, heed his Word, and to do it? The answer to that is, "Yes! It is that difficult!" The people finally listened—the whole remnant. They

The people finally listened.

heard God and his prophet Haggai. I think that means every human being in Jerusalem heard and began to obey God's voice spoken through Haggai. That is all he wanted or expected then, and it is all he wants and expects from us today to hear and obey.

Here comes the turnabout. God takes them from the woodshed (with a good old fashioned whupping) to incredible promise and blessing. Now that they were finally listening, God makes this incredible, reassuring statement: "I am with you, says the LORD," in verse 13. These were God's chosen people. *He* allowed them to be exiled to Babylon, once again to get their attention. Convinced they might have finally got it, *he* sends them back home to rebuild his house. That didn't work either. So God brings even more judgment and wrath and whuppings. But then this loving God reminds them once again: "Hey, gang, I did all of this to remind you that you are mine. I love you and I want what's best for you personally and as a nation."

The Promise Keeper

God is the ultimate promise keeper. He certainly showed this with his great love and watchful care over Israel and Judah. He preserved them even though it wasn't always fun (for either Jehovah or for the children of Israel) because he had promised them he would do so.

The LORD appeared to him [Isaac] on the night of his arrival [in Beersheba]. "I am the God of your father, Abraham," he said.

"Do not be afraid, for I am with you and will bless you. I will multiply your descendants, and they will become a great nation. I will do this because of my promise to Abraham, my servant." (Gen. 26:24 NLT)

God promised again that he loved them, that he would bless them, and that he would preserve them. All he wanted in return was for them to listen and obey.

Another clear promise is the word of Jeremiah to the remnant in chapter 15 verses 19-20.

This is how the Lord responds:

"If you return to me, I will restore you
so you can continue to serve me.
If you speak good words rather than worthless ones,
you will be my spokesman.
You must influence them;
do not let them influence you!
They will fight against you like an attacking army, but I will make
you as secure as a fortified wall of bronze.
They will not conquer you,
for I am with you to protect and rescue you.
I, the Lord, have spoken!" (NLT)

Throughout the Old and New Testaments God calls us to be wise and generous stewards, and to obey. He promises us—and Israel and Judah—great benefits by keeping this lofty goal of obedience. He will keep his covenant. He wants us to be Obedient Owners.

Pop rocker and long time singer Bob Dylan wrote and sang a song on one of his albums during his brief adventure into the

Christian realm in the early 80's with the lyrics "God don't make promises that he don't keep." Dylan, perhaps somewhat unaware, was singing about the theme of the Old, and for that matter, the New, Testament. Through God's Son Jesus, we believers are promised salvation and eternal life. God is the ultimate promise keeper. This fact is an ongoing core value of both the Old and New Testament. God will keep his Word!

"God don't make promises he don't keep."

His promise here in Haggai is clear. If the children of Israel would heed the call and rebuild the temple, God would bless them. He would protect them. The prophet closes the book with a Messianic oracle to jog the memory of Israel once again that God loves them. This prophetic vision delivered by Haggai is a reminder. "My spirit remains among you, just as I promised when you came out of Egypt" (Hag. 2:5 NLT). Another Messianic word from Jehovah stated, "From this day onward I will bless you" (Haggai 2:19b NLT). God promised them land, deliverance, safety—and his hand of blessing upon them. This Messianic prediction is confirmed throughout these 38 verses.

This covenant is made good on the part of the people when they can say of everything they have, "It ain't mine." This fact is made clear throughout scripture and throughout this book. The psalmist asks the ownership question in this way: "What can I offer the Lord for all He has done for me?" (Ps. 116:12 NLT) By now I hope both Haggai and I have answered it: "EVERYTHING."

That's stewardship. Even though the Israelites here in Haggai did not want to be stewards, they had no choice. God commanded them, and then he demanded that they fall into line and acknowledge his power and authority in their lives.

Douglas John Hall said stewardship is a "biblical image come of age." Disobedient ownership and ego was the image of those whom Haggai addressed, and it is the same for many of us today. By the way, a great acrostic and perhaps definition of ego is *Edging God Out*. The clash of these powerful images—the owner and the steward—caused a great dilemma for the Jerusalem residents in 522 BC, and they cause a great dilemma in our consumer culture of 2011. Is the basic role of my life to be an owner or a steward? It's very clear to me as a child of God, I have no choice but to grow and mature and seek to become a true biblical steward. If I choose not to do so, the promise is very clear.

---

[11] Blackaby, Henry T., and Richard Blackaby. *Experiencing God Day-by-Day: A Devotional.* New York, NY: Walker, 2000, p. 220.
[12] Blackaby, p. 220.

5

A Nation Comes to Grips: Tipping God

"Personal finance is 80% behavior and 20% head knowledge." — Dave Ramsey

"Failure is the opportunity to begin more intelligently." — Henry Ford

Imagine this scenario at your local church next Sunday.

We exit your church at 12:15 p.m. after a rousing sermon on love. The sermon title was, "It's all Greek to Me," a study of the three love words: Philos, Eros, and Agape. (Wow! That's good stuff. I should preach that sermon sometime.) Pat and Jane are visiting your church and we agree to go out to dinner (our treat) with six of your friends. With you and us that makes ten. We all go down to the local Outback Steak House (one of my favorites) for a bit of post-church food, fun, and fellowship.

We order dinner from a great—and I mean great!—waiter. We order bloomin' onions, shrimp on the barbie, individual meals, coffee, dessert; and he delivers everything hot and fast as he tells funny stories and meets our every dining need. The food was good, the fellowship was great, and the bill was just over $200.00.

How much should I tip the server? It's a fair question, one that every one of us has asked ourselves over the years. For poor service 5% is my minimum, for fair service 10% seems right, for good service we tip 15%, and for great service we tip 20%. We had just experienced great service! Hence, the tip (for you non-math majors) is slightly more than $40.00.

What's my point?

We just tipped the server at Outback 20%. But, according to The Barna Research Group, some of us ten guests sitting at the table left church one and a half hours earlier and tipped God only 5% when the plate was passed! Is there something wrong with this picture? We tipped 15% more to the server than we shared at church with the God who saved us and provided salvation freely in his redemptive plan

We need to give out of a heart of love.

through Jesus? Certainly we must not think of tipping God for good service. We need to give out of a heart of love and gratitude.

Ground Rules

Most of us understand it is customary to tip those who serve us, to give a little extra money as an acknowledgement of good work. The ground rules of tipping according to Emily Post and other etiquette authorities tell us the size of the tip can depend upon these factors:

- The quality of service
- The frequency of service
- How long you have used the service provider
- Regional custom
- Your budget
- Your spirit of generosity

Who do we tip on a regular or at least an annual basis (perhaps during the Christmas Season)?
- Food Service Workers
- Hairdressers or Barbers
- Manicurists
- Beauticians
- Personal Trainers
- Massage Therapists
- Baby Sitters
- House Cleaners
- Lawn Care Crew
- Pool Cleaners
- Pet Groomers

This is by no means an exhaustive list, but you get the picture. We are tippers here in America—but are we tithers and givers?

According to George Barna and others who research giving patterns in America, the percentage of giving to the local church last year based on joint family income is as follows:
- In Liturgical Churches: 2-3%
- In Main Line Denominations: 4-5%
- In Charismatic Churches and Cults: 7-8%

If 10% is the benchmark for tithing in our churches according to the Bible, we missed it last year.

These Jerusalem dwellers in Haggai began "tipping God" fourteen years prior, then they just stopped giving altogether—no time, no talent, and certainly no treasure.

The Lilly Endowment conducted a Congregational Giving Study in 1997 and discovered the annual contributions US households made to the five major denominations.[13] Factoring in inflation, here's what the numbers would look like in 2011:

- Assemblies of God $2,176
- Southern Baptist $1,504
- Presbyterian USA $1,385
- Evangelical Lutheran Church $956
- Roman Catholic $486

Could I hear someone say, "I am amazed that the average US household in the Assembly of God denomination last year made a salary of only $22,000?" Or, "A whole lot of Southern Baptists made only $15,000 in annual compensation last year." This is what we would assume if we believe people are actually tithing to their churches. It is obvious we are not coming close to giving to God (through our local churches) what we give to those who provide even the most mediocre services at our restaurants and salons.

Obviously, the comparisons to tipping a service provider are really there only to suggest that many of us don't assign our resources according to the things we say we care about, at least when it comes to money. The point is not so much about quibbling over what percentage of our income we give to the church or other ministry compared to what we give to a waiter. Rather, is what we give truly representative of a "love debt," the recognition that we are simply stewards of what God has entrusted to us along with the far more significant gift of salvation? If we feel that love debt, and truly desire to be Obedient Owners, then giving generously and not holding back from the first fruits of our labors will be the demonstration of our commitment.

Déjà Vu All Over Again

God acknowledges the low tip he was receiving from the people.

It's because of you that the heavens withhold the dew and the earth produces no crops. I have called for a drought on your fields and hills—a drought to wither the grain and grapes and olive trees and all your other crops, a drought to starve you and your livestock and to ruin everything you have worked so hard to get. (Hag. 1:10-11 NLT)

The outlook of traditional Covenant Theology holds that faithfulness to God brings blessings on the land and its inhabitants. Disobedience brings just the opposite impact as we see in these two verses.[14] Obedient ownership is God's perfect stewardship strategy.

God answered their lack of giving, their lack of trying, and their lack of obedience with a solemn message. "You are starving physically and spiritually because I want to compensate you as you have compensated me."

Hoarding

Remember the three T's from Chapter 2—our time, our talents, and our treasure. Only one has the capability of being controlled and hoarded—our treasure. This is important and worth repeating.

We cannot hoard our time, and we cannot manipulate time; time marches on. A talent is given to us to be used and cannot be hoarded.

But treasure can be, and often is, hoarded.

But treasure can be, and often is, hoarded. We can stockpile it, handle it, and make the declaration that it is mine.

Of the three T's, only treasure can be possessed and stock-piled.

---

[13] McNamara, Patrick & Zech, Charles. Lagging Stewards. *America,* September 14, 1996, p. 9-15.

[14] The Cambridge Bible Commentary—Haggai, Zechariah, & Malachi. Cambridge Press, 1977, p. 14.

6

Dare to Compare:
Feast or Famine

"Visions are easy to criticize ... Visions attract criticism ... Visions are difficult to defend against criticism ... Visions often die at the hands of critics." — Andy Stanley

"Vision without action is a daydream ... action without vision is a nightmare."
— Japanese Proverb

Chapter 2 of Haggai begins with the Jewish exiles being in the midst of The Feast of Tabernacles. This was a commemorative feast; the dwelling in booths in memory of God's bringing them out of Egypt. This was the seventh day of the feast; the very next day they were to celebrate the Sabbath.

As fun as it sounds, the feasters were probably not in a good mood. They had to be depressed as they reflected upon God's deliverance of Israel from the hand of Pharaoh all those years ago compared to the utter despair that was their lot in life at the moment. They were hungry, cold, discouraged, and flat broke. They were celebrating the feast but preparing to go back to the reality of their current spiritual, economic, and cultural famine.

> *They were hungry, discouraged, and flat broke.*

Can I hear an "Amen" from the congregation? This sounds like our current world! This is the world Haggai is sent to prophesy to. Don't you know he must have said, "Thanks, God! How could it get any worse?" His task was to get them out of the famine mentality. His call was one of faithfulness and fruitfulness. He had stirred them up and they were ready to get after it.

The Good Old Days

David's temple was a wonder of the world 600+ years before the birth of Christ. Its beauty and splendor were unsurpassed. It was not just a holy place but a worship center of incredible size and beauty. Marble, stone, gold, silver, and bronze adorned David's temple throughout. It was literally breathtaking, causing people to gasp when they saw it. Its beauty prepared their hearts for worship of Jehovah.

Think about some of those wonders of our existing world that you may have personally observed: The Great Wall of China, the Grand Canyon, the view from the Empire State Building, Niagara Falls, the Sphinx, and the Pyramids. You will never forget the grandeur, the size, and the fact that all the digital photos you can take will not do justice to these sites. This is the introduction to Haggai's second prophetic message.

Then on October 17 of that same year, the Lord sent another message through the prophet Haggai. "Say this to Zerubbabel son of Shealtiel, governor of Judah, and to Jeshua son of Jehozadak, the high priest, and to the remnant of God's people there in the land: 'Does anyone remember this house—this Temple—in its former splendor? How, in comparison, does it look to you now? It must seem like nothing at all!'" (Hag. 2:1-3 NLT)

Let's do some math, to get a perspective. The temple was destroyed around 587 BC. The Babylonians did not leave one rock standing. The beautiful temple of David was totally destroyed. Now it's 520 BC. That's 67 years later. Just to set the stage, let's say someone was ten years old when he went into captivity at the hands of the Babylonians; that individual would now be seventy-seven years old. He would certainly remember; how could he forget such grandeur? And it would be clear the partially built temple before him now couldn't even begin to be compared to the temple of his youth.

Perhaps Haggai may have been one of those older Jews who saw the former temple. Regardless, Haggai admits to the people the poverty of this new building compared to the former temple. But in spite of this he will encourage them to stay engaged and keep working, as we will see in just a couple of verses. Since many of those working on this new scaled down temple had never seen David's temple, it was just word of mouth from those mature exilers.

Haggai and his boss Jehovah want the exiles to be obedient and rebuild. They don't expect the new temple to be as glorious or magnificent as the former temple. David and Solomon had lots more resources to work with. But Jehovah is going to be glorified in this new temple built out of wood, not marble.

Ezra 3:10-14 mentions "great rejoicing" and "weeping for joy" by those who returned to Jerusalem fourteen years earlier and who had helped lay the foundation of the new temple. We are not told if the rejoicing was because they envisioned a temple that would rival David and Solomon's.

It is very likely that the descriptions most of the fifty thousand exiles had regarding the former temple were by word of mouth, not from personal experience. Still, they would have heard over and over from those who were there, "It's not going to be as great as David's and Solomon's version. Don't you remember its beauty and grandeur?"

I frankly wonder sometimes if the good old days were really that good.

My father has passed on, but I remember table discussions where he talked about walking five miles to school, up hill both ways, almost always in the snow. However, I checked many years ago and found out that Joplin, Missouri, averages only about five inches of snow annually.

Perhaps those listening to the stories about the original temple wondered if it really had been all that magnificent.

Still, the vision caught on, thanks to Haggai. The people caught the passion, a call, a commitment to move forward with building a temple.

Moving Forward

Up to now there had been very little courage or conviction on the part of the priests, the princes, or the people. That was about to change.

But now the Lord says: Be strong, Zerubbabel. Be strong, Je-shua son of Jehozadak, the high priest. Be strong, all you people still left in the land. And now get to work, for I am with you, says the Lord of Heaven's Armies. My Spirit remains among you, just as I promised when you came out of Egypt. So do not be afraid. (Hag. 2:5-6 NLT)

This passage speaks for itself. Jehovah reminds them *he* is with them and they should take courage and should not be afraid. Haggai helps them connect with their Jewish history and heritage as they were just finishing up seven days of celebrating The Feast of Tabernacles. Although during the previous fourteen years they showed no desire to be courageous in their faith, nor did they appear to be listening to Jehovah, that had now changed.

The awesome part of God's unfailing love is clearly shared in this statement. "My Spirit has been and always will be with you, Oh Israel and Judah. I loved you and was with you then and now." Even though God had judged them by allowing them to be exiled, he loved them. Even though part of God's judgment upon Israel and Judah was to punish them by dividing them as a nation, he never stopped loving them.

They showed no desire to be courageous in their faith.

At this time in our world it is very comforting to know that God loves me and he is still in charge of world affairs, the economy, my meager stock account, our children and granddaughter—you know, all the "small" stuff.

Once again, Haggai, speaking the word of Jehovah, reminds the Jews of their covenant relationship. "This is what the Lord Almighty says" shows up throughout the temple rebuilding books of the Old Testament. The Haggai passage reads this way:

For this is what the LORD of Heaven's Armies says: In just a little while I will again shake the heavens and the earth, the oceans and the dry land. I will shake all the nations, and the treasures of all the nations will be brought to this Temple. I will fill this place with glory, says the LORD of Heaven's Armies. The silver is mine, and the gold is mine, says the LORD of Heaven's Armies. The future glory of this Temple will be greater than its past glory, says the LORD of Heaven's Armies. And in this place I will bring peace. I, the LORD of Heaven's Armies, have spoken! (Hag. 2:6-9 NLT)

The Lord declares "in a little while," and most commentators liken this to a Messianic promise that it is just 520 years until the birth of Christ. In light of eternity, it is very likely Haggai understood this is a mere moment in God's timing.

A Whole Lot of Shakin' Goin' On

As for shaking the earth, God has done it before and will do it again during the tribulation and at the end of the millennium. I wonder if Pharaoh, the greatest earthly leader of his time all those years before, would admit that Jehovah, the God of Israel, shook up his world. Jehovah sent ten plagues, each more devastating than the last, and concluded with every male child not covered by the covenant being killed in a single night (Ex. 7-11). Pharaoh's world was shaken so hard he released Moses and the captive Jews to pursue their lives in the land Jehovah had promised to them.

Here Haggai's statement, "I will once more shake" seems to be an overview of God's past and future judgment upon the world. He has the power and authority to shake up any nation, including the United States of America and our current and future economic "shake down."

Think through the shaking that has taken place throughout the Bible. The entire known world was shaken by the flood; only Noah and his family and a big boat full of animals survived. Persia, Greece, and Rome were all shaken prior to the birth of Christ. Haggai is sharing the supreme control of God among the nations, who uses the shaking for the advancement of his own kingdom. The scripture is chock full of prophecy and prediction.

Old Testament scholar E.B. Pusey has this to say about God's shaking surrounding the coming and second coming of the Messiah.

"Prophecy, in its long perspective, uses a continual foreshortening, speaking of things in relation to their eternal meaning and significance, as to that which shall survive, when heaven and earth and even time shall have passed away. It blends together the beginning and the earthly end; the preparation and the result; the commencement of redemption and its completion;

our Lord's coming in humility [Bethlehem] and in His Majesty [second coming]....The Seed of the woman, Who should bruise the serpent's head, was promised on the fall; to Abraham, the blessing through his seed; by Moses, the prophet like unto him; to David, an everlasting covenant. Joel unites the out-pouring of the Spirit of God on the Day of Pentecost, and the hatred of the world till the Day of Judgment; Isaiah, god's judgments on the land and the Day of final judgment; the deliverance from Babylon, and the first coming of Christ; the glories of the Church, the new heavens and the new earth which shall remain forever."[15]

Suffice to say, God reminds them and us that he has the power to shake nations, and cause GM stock to tank, and bring great companies and great nations to their knees. He wants Judea to be reminded of that incredible, awesome authority on a planet that he created.

Commentary writers Keil and Delitzch reinforce the Messianic prophecy of Haggai in this quotation.

God reminds them and us that he has the power to shake the earth.

"The desired of all nations shall come and I will fill this house with glory [Haggai 2:7]." Is this a question about the promise of the coming Messiah? It certainly seems to be. In the year 520 B.C. when the ten tribes had already been scattered among the heathen for 200 years and Judeans for more than seventy years, the Messianic hope of Israel could not be any longer altogether unknown to the nations. This seems to be a prophetic reference to the glorification of the temple through the appearance of Jesus in it. The fulfillment of prophecy did commence with the fact that Jehovah came to His temple in the person of Jesus Christ.[16]

In Malachi 3:1 this is confirmed with this statement:

"Look! I am sending my messenger, and he will prepare the way before me. Then the LORD you are seeking will suddenly come to his Temple. The messenger of the covenant, whom you look for so eagerly, is surely coming," says the LORD of Heaven's Armies. (NLT)

Haggai was clearly reminding this Jewish remnant that the promised Messiah (the one who would redeem and deliver Israel) would return to the temple—not this temple, but another temple sometime in the future. This passage seems to have a dual meaning or application both to Jehovah's promise to "fill this place with his glory" right now, and a promise of another temple where Israel (God's chosen people) would be restored.

The Good, the Bad, and the Ugly

Thankfully, there is more good news than bad and ugly in this passage, but all three are there. In light of the judgment that had fallen on Judah, Jehovah's promise is excellent news to them. Verse 7 concludes with the promise to fill this temple and the temple in the future with glory. Remember the old hymn we sang some years ago?

When we walk with the Lord in the light of his Word,
What a glory he sheds on our way!
While we do his good will, he abides with us still,
And with all who will trust and obey.

It's the old hymn "Trust and Obey," something Israel had not done for two hundred years or so. I have often wondered what the phrase, "what a glory he sheds on our way" really means. I think it is a promise to bless every aspect of their lives and ours—our time, our talent, our treasure, our children, our home life, our jobs, our service in the church and to mankind. Jehovah promised them and us that he will fill our lives with his glory if we will allow him to do so. All we must do is be "sold out" Obedient Owners. This is good news!

Israel and Judah had been in captivity two hundred years and seventy years, respectively. When they were captured and exiled, the invasion forces always stole their valuables.

What a glory he sheds on our way.

Much of their gold and silver had been looted and was in the hands of foreign governments. The original temple had been totally overlaid in gold; all of the bowls and chalices had been silver. Those were missing; but Jehovah reminded them that while they did not know where all of that stuff was, he did. The bowls were in the possession of the Hittites, the Babylonians had a lot of the silver, even the Assyrians and many others had valuables from the temple and the inhabitants of Jerusalem.

For obvious reasons this was bad, at least for now.

Bold statement from Jehovah! "It's all mine, the silver and the gold. And I know where it is. At the appointed time I will restore your riches and wealth." Jehovah reminds them that he can recover all of those valuables when he is ready, or perhaps when these Jewish exiles have proven that they are ready. They are finally ready to be "obedient owners" of God's glorious promises and covenants.

Guess what? Here is an admonition for our world today in the middle of an economic meltdown: It's all God's stuff and he can take it back, reduce it, or make it disappear at any moment.

The brightest and best on Wall Street, on Main Street, and in our government have been proven totally wrong. Their predictions and recommendations have been like a child's in light of God's authority here on earth and His "yea verily" in economic and financial strategies. Perhaps the quicker we admit this and honor God with our finances, the sooner there will be an eternal economic stimulus package.

That God reminds people of his ownership is the good part. The bad and very ugly part is our attempt to take ownership ourselves these past 3,000 years here in our world. Obedient Owners manage according to the will of the owner, Jehovah!

My interpretation of verse 9 starts out with ugly. Downsizing is something we understand here in America. For economic, personal, or generational purposes we downsize from a 3,000 square foot home to an 1,800 square foot condo—big-to-small, or at least smaller. That is what Judah was doing here. They were doing a rebuild on the temple David and Solomon built. Even in the euphoria of the moment they understood it was going to be inferior, as it was constructed out of wood, not gold or marble or precious stones, and didn't have silver goblets. It was ugly by comparison.

Haggai, speaking for God, shares an incredible promise with them. "'The glory of this present house will be greater than the glory of the former house,' says the LORD Almighty" (Hag. 2:8 NIV). By continually making these "Lord Almighty" statements (or "the LORD of Heaven's Armies" according to the NLT) to his people, the Jews, God seems to be reminding them of this fact: He is directing their paths and this temple project. Haggai addresses their existing circumstances and accordingly promises that future glorification of the temple will outshine the glory of the former one. The Lord God will one day exalt his kingdom (which was so deeply degraded and despised) to a glory that will far surpass the glory of the kingdom of God at the time of Solomon—because all the heathen nations will dedicate their possessions to it.

And that's really what it is all about.

New and Improved

Let's see what Keil and Delitzsch have to say about the new and improved house of God.

This glorification of the house of God wasn't because the wood and stone magically turned into precious jewels. In fact, the temple built by Haggai and the crew, and subsequently finished by Herod, fell into ruins because the Jews had rejected their Savior and crucified him. This glorification of the house of God commenced with the introduction of the kingdom of heaven, which Jesus Christ preached and by which he laid the foundation of his church. The spreading of the kingdom of God among the nations of the earth will be completed at the end of the course of this world—not by the erection of a new and much more glorious temple in Jerusalem, but in the founding of the new Jerusalem coming down out of heaven from God upon the new earth, after the overthrow of all the powers of the world that are hostile to God and to his chosen people Israel.[17]

In 520 BC, Jehovah encouraged the people to keep building because this house of God will be a place of God's glory. This wooden rebuild and remodeling job will be recognized by God as greater than the temple David and Solomon constructed. That's exactly what the prophet Haggai said to the people. God is honoring their faithfulness to rise up and rebuild the temple. He is pleased with their obedience.

This is good news—but it gets even better.

As Haggai closes out this second message, he makes an incredible statement. "And in this place I will bring peace. I, the LORD of Heaven's Armies, have spoken" (2:9 NLT). What is our world looking for? It's looking for peace! Once again, there appears to be a twofold interpretation of this passage. Jehovah will bring peace both to Judah for their faithfulness and obedience in the temple project and to the Gentiles through the cross. Author Davidson helps us understand this peace.

The deep-seated need of man will be met—peace. This place is first of all Jerusalem, the place where God's house stands. But the vision is widened for us today. The Prince of Peace has come to earth. Haggai and many other Old Testament passages announce the birth of Jesus. On His authority we know that neither in this place nor yet in Jerusalem shall men worship.

The spiritual temple of God is everywhere and peace still has its home there.[18]

The apostle Paul made this very clear in his epistle to the Ephesians.

Together as one body, Christ reconciled both groups to God by means of his death on the cross, and our hostility toward each other was put to death. He brought this Good News of peace to you Gentiles who were far away from him, and peace to the Jews who were near. (Eph. 2:16-17 NLT)

Peace and prosperity would, in part, be the children of Israel's existence for the next 520 years (with the exception of the Roman-occupation) before the birth of Christ.

This also is very good.

Haggai got the troops cranked up in a very short period of time. Everyone was in agreement. (Imagine that in your local church or organizational context!) All of the exiled Jews put their shoulder to the project. Amazing things can happen when we all get together and get after it! So concludes Haggai's second message to the people.

---

[15] Pusey, E B. *The Minor Prophets: With a Commentary, Explanatory and Practical, and Introductions to the Several Books, Volume II.* Nabu Press, 2010, p. 309-310.

[16] Keil, Carl F, and Franz Delitzsch. *Commentary on the Old Testament in Ten Volumes.* Grand Rapids, MI: Wm. B. Eerdmans, 1983, p. 485.

[17] Keil & Delitzsch, p. 490.

[18] Davidson, Francis. *The New Bible Commentary.* Grand Rapids, MI: Wm. B. Eerdmans, 1960, p. 746.

7

Clean or Dirty

"Nothing can be more cruel than the leniency which abandons others to their sin. Nothing can be more compassionate than the severe reprimand which calls another Christian to one's community back from the path of sin."
— **Dietrich Bonhoeffer**

As part of his series on stewardship and lifestyle giving, Haggai shared with the temple rebuilders a third sermon that begins with a bit of a conundrum. The big question he addresses is how to get clean after being defiled. Haggai begins this narrative with a couple of questions, this time to the Priests. (Remember the entire book had admonitions to the Princes, the People, and the Priests.)

Q&A #1

Approximately two months after the previous sermon and three months out from the temple foundation being laid, Haggai is at it again. He is the mouthpiece of Jehovah and has asked a couple of "yea" or "nay" questions. He's not initiating a dialogue; he's looking for just a thumbs-up or thumbs-down.

Ask the priests what the law says: If a person carries consecrated meat in the fold of his garment, and that fold touches some bread or stew, some wine, oil or other food, does it become consecrated? (Hag. 2:11-12 NIV)

The priest's point of reference to the question (clean or dirty) was to go back to the Torah, the Law of Moses. Here was their perspective: "You must distinguish between what is sacred and what is common, between what is ceremonially unclean and what is clean. And you must teach the Israelites all the decrees that the LORD has given them through Moses" (Lev. 10:10-11 NLT).

SURVEY SAYS.................No! Based upon the law of Moses, the answer to Haggai's question was NO! In a New York second the priest got it right.

Q&A #2

Haggai presents another question.

Then Haggai said, "If a person defiled by contact with a dead body touches one of these things, does it become defiled?"
"Yes," the priests replied, "it becomes defiled."

Then Haggai said, "'So it is with this people and this nation in my sight,' declares the LORD. 'Whatever they do and whatever they offer there is defiled.'" (Hag. 2:13-14 NIV)

God's comparison of his people to something defiled was a serious judgment upon this nation. Numbers 19 sheds some additional light upon this contamination. "Anyone out in the open who touches someone who has been killed with a sword or someone who has died a natural death, or anyone who touches a human bone or a grave, will be unclean for seven days" (Num. 19:16 NIV). The passage goes on in verse 22 to define the impact of this defilement. "Anything that an unclean person touches becomes unclean, and anyone who touches it becomes unclean till evening" (NIV).

Bad Eggs

The Priests answered Haggai's questions out of their understanding and practice of the law. Everything that disobedient Israel/Judah touched became contaminated. The nation was defiled, and everything they touched or did became defiled as well. The sin of disobedience seems to spread faster, quicker, and deeper than righteousness. The possession of a holy thing does not counterbalance disobedience.

James, one of the New Testament contributors, defines it well when he says, "For the person who keeps all of the laws except one is as guilty as a person who has broken all of God's laws" (James 2:10 NLT).

The nation was "dirty" and could not figure out how to get clean on its own. They tried!

The nation was dirty and could not figure out how to get clean on its own.

Our friend's dog, Diesel, surprised a skunk a month ago. Diesel's owners tried tomato juice, soap of every kind, and other recommended concoctions. Diesel himself rubbed himself raw in spots to try to get rid of the odor, and he still smelled for nearly a week. He was defiled, and those around him for a period felt defiled as well. Haggai was saying essentially what our grandmothers used to say to us: "One bad egg spoils the whole omelet."

Haggai is setting up the people for a divine blessing, a promise. This divine promise is not restricted, however, to the act of divine service undertaken in obedience to the call of God. After more than fourteen years of disobedience they began to rebuild the temple. Once the foundation of the new temple was laid, three months after the work began, Haggai gave to the people the further encouragement that they would begin to experience Jehovah's hand of blessing. As long as the land stood under the desecration of a ruined and abandoned temple, everything was made unclean.

Haggai is setting up the people for a divine blessing

While one holy object does not sanctify other defiled objects, that which is unclean does have a contagious quality by which it corrupts everything it touches. Fear and negativity sometimes trumps faithfulness. Apathy sometimes wins over obedience and a get-it-done-no-matter-how-difficult-it is attitude.

In the case of Judah (mentioned here in Haggai), the ruined and neglected temple had become a canker, a national cancer which affected every aspect of the peoples' daily lives. Although they tried to make their lives successful, Jehovah was thwarting the fruits of their labor (their cattle, their crops, their money, their homes, their schools, their entire beings) because of their disobedience.

These two very important questions, both designed to help the exiles see the error of their ways, were answered correctly by the Priests. Obedience triggers God's divine blessings, both then and now. It's once again that obedient ownership deal.

Never Forget

How quickly we forget. We have short-term memories, and perhaps that's good. The people's situation was bad; however it was getting better, and there was hope it might even get good again. Haggai is setting us up for his fourth sermon (given on the same day) and a truly divine stimulus package and promise.

> *"Now give careful thought to this from this day on—consider how things were before one stone was laid on another in the LORD's temple. When anyone came to a heap of twenty measures, there were only ten. When anyone went to a wine vat to draw fifty measures, there were only twenty. I struck all the work of your hands with blight, mildew and hail, yet you did not turn to me,' declares the LORD. From this day on, from this twenty-fourth day of the ninth month, give careful thought to the day when the foundation of the LORD's temple was laid. Give careful thought: Is there yet any seed left in the barn? Until now, the vine and the fig tree, the pomegranate and the olive tree have not borne fruit. "From this day on I will bless you."'* (Hag. 2:15-19 NIV)

Do verses 16-17 sound familiar, like the front page of today's Wall Street Journal, or the recent call from your broker or your boss? Economic downturn on steroids! Their recession/depression went way beyond belt tightening; they didn't even have a belt to tighten. High unemployment, shrinking investments, even the rainy day fund (the grain and the oil) vaporized.

Haggai wants them to remember their disobedient past, but also that there is light at the end of the tunnel. The prophet proves his thesis by references to the social, economic, and spiritual difficulties experienced by the people, so long as the temple was left in ruins. Now that they had begun to rebuild, he assures

Their recession/ depression went way beyond belt tightening.

them their economic problems will come to an end. Haggai reminds them of the date in order that there should be no doubt as to their obedience to rebuild the temple and God's divine plan to rebuild their social, spiritual, and economic portfolios. This will be a divine blessing, because Jehovah is going to increase what is not really there. They had used all of their reserves while in survival mode, but God promises to bless them! Those blessings are the

result of the steps of obedience the people took by rebuilding the House of God.

Yes friends, Jehovah Jirah (my provider) oversees the economic blessings of this world. When you are obedient to him, he'll provide for you—whether you use the yen, the pound, the euro, the peso, the yuan, the rupee, the dinar, the dollar, or the schilling.

8

The Divine Promises

*"You're blessed when you stay on course,
walking steadily on the road revealed by God.
You're blessed when you follow his directions,
doing your best to find him."*
(Psalm 119:1 The Message)

The fourth message took place on the same day as the third message. Haggai got rolling and just could not stop. Maybe your pastor does it too—the sermon is so good, he just keeps going. In this final message are a number of promises that Haggai announces to Zerubbabel and the people. If you need the Cliff Notes, here is a list of the promises in verses 20-23 that God makes to Zerubbabel. Jehovah promises to

- Shake the heavens and the earth
- Overturn royal thrones

- Shatter the power of foreign kingdoms
- Overthrow chariots
- Overthrow drivers
- Overthrow horses
- Overthrow riders
- Turn Judah's enemies against each other
- Make Zerubbabel like his signet ring

Three verses and lots of promises. And God never fails to keep his word. I think there is an object lesson floating around in there somewhere. What if our modern-day Princes (political leaders), Priests (religious leaders), and People (us, the laity) would carefully and prayerfully consider each and every promise in God's word? Living our lives as Obedient Owners, our world would be a very different place. If our world functioned that way, it would be like this:

> *God never fails to keep his word.*

A deep sense of awe came over them all, and the apostles performed many miraculous signs and wonders. And all the believers met together in one place and shared everything they had. They sold their property and possessions and shared the money with those in need. They worshiped together at the Temple each day, met in homes for the Lord's Supper, and shared their meals with great joy and generosity—all the while praising God and enjoying the goodwill of all the people. And each day the Lord added to their fellowship those who were being saved. (Acts 2:43-47 NLT)

This is not socialism or revisionism, this is theocracy at its finest hour.

The Promise to Preserve and Protect

Haggai concludes with a special message to the governor Zerubbabel, who has taken the lead in response to the prophetic and stewardship summons. At a time of confusion and change among the nations living in and around Jerusalem, Zerubbabel was confirmed in his position as the divinely elected leader of the people. The parallel is clear to the Promised (there's that word again) Messiah being summoned to earth to build a temple not made with hands, who will remain when all earthly kingdoms and governments are shaken and overthrown.

The word of the LORD came to Haggai a second time on the twenty-fourth day of the month: "Tell Zerubbabel governor of Judah that I will shake the heavens and the earth. I will overturn royal thrones and shatter the power of the foreign kingdoms. I will overthrow chariots and their drivers; horses and their riders will fall, each by the sword of his brother." (Hag. 2:20-21 NIV)

If the definition of prophecy is a prediction of the future made under divine inspiration, then Haggai was a prophet and these verses are prophesy. It's a future event brought into the reality of the moment. Once again Jehovah renews the promise of salvation to his chosen people who are rebuilding the second temple in Jerusalem. The prophecy to the community was the preservation and care of the Davidic monarchy, represented for the time by Zerubbabel in the midst of the storms that were about to burst upon the power of the world.[19]

Whole Lot of Shaking Going On

In spite of the international upheaval both then and now, God's promises can be trusted. A renewal of the promise from verses 2:6-7 is stated: "I will once more shake the heavens and the earth, the sea and the dry land" (NIV). Written some six hundred years later is another promise of a world-shaking event. It's in John's book of Revelation where chapter seven reads:

> *Then I saw another angel coming up from the east, having the seal of the living God. He called out in a loud voice to the four angels who had been given power to harm the land and the sea: "Do not harm the land or the sea or the trees until we put a seal on the foreheads of the servants of our God." Then I heard the number of those sealed: 144,000 from all the tribes of Israel.*
> (Rev. 7:2-4 NIV)

These passages are nearly identical, both referencing the promised Messiah who will shake the heavens and the earth, defeat all enemies, and establish his kingdom here on earth. Heady stuff, but both supportive of the same promise—the promise of God's chosen one, Jesus Christ, the Savior of the world.

With this general promise given to the people (shaking of the nations), a particular assurance is given to Zerubbabel who had been first summoned to undertake this rebuilding project and lead the people back to Jehovah. He is told that the time of instability that began with Darius' reign would continue. Neither political nor military security is to be expected among the nations, for God himself is at work to overrule and judge. But Zerubbabel was not to fear, even though his position seemed to be weak by human reckoning, for he had been chosen and established by Jehovah himself. God will have the final say and there will be a whole lot of shaking going on.[20]

The Promised Messiah

Jesus came through the Davidic bloodline. Zerubbabel was of that same bloodline. He returned from captivity sixteen years before as the representative of the house of David and heir to the Davidic covenant. The great promise of salvation and deliverance was to come through David and Zerubbabel and reach on through their descendants to Christ. The Messiah was to return as the King of Kings and the Lord of Lords amid all the overthrow of nations, kingdoms, and rulers. He was to redeem and deliver his people. The gentiles were to be grafted into God's family, become partakers of the grace of God through the Lord Jesus.[21]

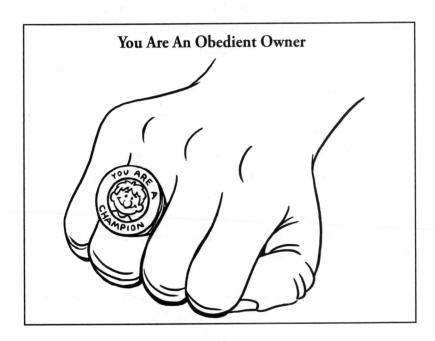

A Signet Ring

"On that day," declares the LORD *Almighty, "I will take you, my servant Zerubbabel son of Shealtiel," declares the* LORD, *"and I will make you like my signet ring, for I have chosen you," declares the* LORD *Almighty.* (Hag. 2:23 NIV)

This final verse of Haggai, like many others, is power packed. It has two significant themes—the current situation and a future reference to the Messiah. Zerubbabel was the Persian governor in Judah, and as son of Shealtiel was a descendant of the family of David. The Messianic promise made to David was transferred to Zerubbabel and his family and culminates in Jesus Christ, the son of David and a descendent of Zerubbabel.

My long time friend and business partner, Dr. Howard Nourse, wears a signet ring received because he was a member of the 1960 Ohio State national champion basketball team. Only 22 of them exist. They were awarded to 15 players, 3 coaches, 3 managers and a team trainer. I can only imagine what an honor it must be to wear such an ornament and be reminded daily of what it represents.

Jehovah promises to present Zerubbabel and his descendant Jesus Christ as a signet ring, an ornament for the entire world to see and appreciate for the reminder it was of his Messianic plan. With the final message of this important minor prophet, the prophecy is given a Messianic range and depth that make it more than the mere illustration of an important truth. As the ruler, called by God to re-build the temple, Zerubbabel foreshadows the "chief cornerstone" of the new spiritual house, Jesus Christ.

Who is prepared for absolute obedience to the divine will even to the point of death? Who is thus enabled to build a temple of surpassing peace and glory and who is established in a kingdom that endures when all the dominions of earth are broken in final judgment? [22]

The book closes the way it opened. It's all about Obedient Ownership. How can we be wise and generous stewards? How can we honor God with our time, our talent, and our treasure? We must manage all of our life according to the will of the owner, Jehovah God, his son Jesus Christ, and under the power and authority of the Holy Spirit.

Haggai's prophecy was an admonition to get your life in order, to consider your ways! The upshot of this prophecy is that political, no less than economic, wellbeing depends ultimately upon a primary readiness to be obedient and to seek God's kingdom and glory. When individuals or nations set themselves to attain material security as a first objective, they condemn themselves to inevitable loss and disappointment. We should know that. We have seen it become a reality in our nation and around the world in this recent economic meltdown.

> *To get your life in order, consider your ways.*

When people are prepared for a first loyalty to Jehovah God and his cause, they can depend upon the gracious provision of God for material and economic needs. Haggai would say five times in a brief conversation with us regarding our economic strategies and practices, "Carefully consider your ways." [23]

Haggai could have written this to his colleagues in Jerusalem in 528 BC:

But seek first his kingdom and his righteousness, and all these things will be given to you as well. Therefore do not worry about tomor-

row, for tomorrow will worry about itself. Each day has enough trouble of its own. (Matt. 6:33-34 NIV)

Read on as Haggai will be joined by all of the other 65 books of the Holy Writ and their perspective on stewardship.

[19] Keil & Delitzsch, p. 497.
[20] Bromiley, Geoffrey W, and Erwin Fahlbusch. *The Encyclopedia of Christianity.* *Vol. 2: Vol. 2 E-I.* Cambridge: Brill-Eerdmans, 2001, p. 751-752.
[21] Pusey, p. 320.
[22] Bromiley, p. 752.
[23] Bromiley, p. 752.

9

The Old Testament Record

"Leaders must challenge the process because systems will unconsciously conspire to maintain the status quo and prevent change."
— The Leadership Challenge

"Then Pharaoh said to Joseph, 'Since God has made all of this known to you, there is no one so discerning and wise as you. You shall be in charge of my palace, and all my people are to submit to your orders. Only with respect to the throne will I be greater than you.'"
(Gen. 41:39-40 NIV)

Haggai had a lot to say about stewardship, as does the entire embodiment of Scripture. The sixty-six books of the Holy Writ are not just about redemption, although that is the most important theme. They are also about stewardship, helping us to become kingdom managers, Obedient Owners. They give clear teaching, training, and discipleship lessons on how to grow and mature in our stewardship practices.

God will hold us accountable for that which he has entrusted to each of us to manage. Stewardship is everything we do after we become a Christian. Remember, it's all God's and he wants us to manage it, help it to grow, and then give it back to him and those around us in the end. Truly following Christ means growing in the grace and knowledge of Christ and becoming a steward—an Obedient Owner.

> *Remember, it's all God's.*

If for some reason you still have the misconception that the Bible doesn't say much about stewardship, please carefully read and study the next two chapters. Every book has a stewardship theme or concept within its narrative—whether it be stewardship of creation (how we manage the resources here on earth), stewardship of relationships (how we enrich the lives of others), stewardship of our mind and bodies, or stewardship of the gospel (how we go about the ministry we are called to be a part of). We are merely Obedient Owners of all those relationships.

I will not get lengthy in my identification of the stewardship concept and principals in the thirty-nine books of the Old Testament—I would encourage you to study all of this a good bit more on your own; I am here simply to get you started on an exciting stewardship tour.

We'll take a brief look at it through the eyes of patriarchs, prophets, kings, princes, a kitchen steward, and a number of shepherds and farmers. Are you ready for a glimpse at the topic of stewardship from bestselling authors like Moses, David, Solomon, Isaiah, Daniel, Haggai, and many others? Here we go on a stewardship journey from Genesis to Malachi.

Genesis

The whole account of creation in Genesis 1-3 was one of stewardship. God created this perfect world and invited its first two inhabitants (Adam and Eve) to manage it. Now, we blew it in Chapter 3, but the first command given to us humans was to take dominion over the fish, the foul, and every living creature.

If you want a verse on tithing just to get us going, Genesis 14:18-20 speaks of how the high priest of God, Melchizedek, blessed Abram with a special blessing from Jehovah. Verse 20 defines Abram's response: "Then Abram gave Melchizedek a tenth of all the goods he had recovered" (NLT).

STEWARDSHIP PRINCIPLE: Our first job description was a stewardship assignment (to wisely manage all of God's creation). It is still our job description today.

Exodus

This book clearly defines the building of the tabernacle, and Moses asks all the children of Israel for an offering from a willing heart.

Tell the people of Israel to bring me their sacred offerings. Accept the contributions from all whose hearts are moved to offer them. Here is a list of sacred offerings you may accept from them: gold, silver and bronze; blue, purple, and scarlet thread; fine linen and goat hair for cloth; tanned ram skins and fine goatskin leather; acacia wood; olive oil for the lamps; spices for the anointing oil and the fragrant incense; onyx stones, and other gemstones to be set in the ephod and the priest's chestpiece. (Ex. 25:2-7 NLT)

By the way, the children of Israel gave so willingly and generously that finally the craftsman left their work to meet with Moses to tell them people were bringing them more than they needed.

Then Moses gave an order and they sent this word throughout the camp: "No man or woman is to make anything else as an offering for the sanctuary." And so the people were restrained from bringing more, because what they already had was more than enough to do all the work. (Ex. 36:6-7 NIV)

Wouldn't you love for that to be the story of your next capital campaign!

STEWARDSHIP PRINCIPLE: Give generously from the heart (from whatever you have) to the point that nothing more is needed.

Leviticus

This is a book about holy living, which is certainly the way to live life as a steward. The word *holy* is used 87 times in these 27 chapters. Moses was reminding God's children to put him first in their lives and live holy lives—and they would be blessed.

Many of the rules and regulations in Leviticus 5:7-11 talk about gifts from those of limited means; they were not off the hook but needed to give what they could.

The word holy *is used 87 times.*

But if you cannot afford to bring a sheep, you must bring to the LORD two turtledoves or two young pigeons as the penalty for your sin. One of the birds will be for a sin offering, and the other for a burnt offering. (Lev. 5:7 NLT)

And:

If you cannot afford to bring two turtledoves or two young pigeons, you may bring two quarts of choice flour for your sin offering. Since it is an offering for sin, you must not moisten it with olive oil or put any frankincense on it. (Lev. 5:11 NLT)

A rule for a thanksgiving offering is also mentioned in chapter 7 verse 12:

If you present your peace offering as an expression of thanksgiving, the usual animal sacrifice must be accompanied by various kinds of bread made without yeast—thin cakes mixed with olive oil, wafers spread with oil, and cakes made of choice flour mixed with olive oil. (Lev. 7:12 NLT)

Aren't you thankful holy living can be achieved today because of the work of the cross, not by keeping the law—which is impossible to do anyway.

STEWARDSHIP PRINCIPLE: Be a holy liver and a holy giver! Seek holiness and your biblical stewardship will become the lifestyle of an Obedient Owner.

Numbers

This is a book of the census. By the very nature of counting the congregation, God is showing that each person is special, unique, and priceless. Love of people, not things, is a huge stewardship concept.

The LORD spoke to Moses in the Tent of Meeting in the Desert of Sinai on the first day of the second month of the second year after the Israelites came out of Egypt. He said: "Take a census of the whole Israelite community by their clans and families, listing every man by name, one by one." (Num. 1:1-2 NIV)

Chapter 7:13-85 is all about stewardship as Moses helped the Levites receive a series of dedication gifts for the tabernacle from the children of Israel.

Jehovah reminded them and us that he is the owner and we need to give our first fruits to him.

Then divide the plunder into two parts, and give half to the men who fought the battle and half to the rest of the people. From the army's portion, first give the LORD his share of the plunder—one of every 500 of the prisoners and of the cattle, donkeys, sheep, and goats. Give this share of the army's half to Eleazar the priest as an offering to the LORD." (Num. 31:27-29 NLT)

God reminded them that the battle they just won was because of his blessing upon them; he wanted them to be faithful stewards in sharing the bounty. God wants us to share our bounty with him as well.

STEWARDSHIP PRINCIPLE: God owns it all and he knows what he has entrusted to us. He wants us to bring our very best to him as our "first fruits."

Deuteronomy

This fifth book of Moses spells stewardship with the three letter word "ALL." Moses encourages all of the stewards to love God with "all your heart and soul" (4:29 NLT). If we will honor God as stewards and heed his commands, he promises that you will "find him."

In the distant future, when you are suffering all these things, you will finally return to the LORD your God and listen to what he tells you. For the LORD your God is a merciful God; he will not abandon you or destroy you or forget the solemn covenant he made with your ancestors. (4:30-31 NLT)

We learn from Deuteronomy that stewardship is not about equal giving but equal sacrifice.

All must give as they are able, according to the blessings given to them by the LORD your God. (Deut. 16:17 NLT)

STEWARDSHIP PRINCIPLE: True stewards honor God the True Owner of all things. As Obedient Owners, they give and live according to the wishes of the owner.

Joshua

Joshua's book is one of faith and courage under fire, a test of our lives as stewards. It is about how to follow God's commands when it's hard, when the enemy is at hand, when the economy goes south. In chapter 3, verse 5 Joshua promises the children of Israel a bright and blessed future: "Purify yourselves, for tomorrow the LORD will do great wonders among you" (NLT).

Ultimately our decision to be a steward is one of choice. The question is answered in the last part of the verse with this statement:

"But if you refuse to serve the LORD, then choose today whom you will serve.... as for me and my family, we will serve the LORD." (Josh. 24:15 NLT)

Our decision to be a steward is one of choice.

STEWARDSHIP PRINCIPLE: The obedience and practice of stewardship can and should be passed along from one generation to the next. Our children are watching!

Judges

The judges who were bathed in righteousness were God's stewards. They were God's managers. Deborah was a wise and righteous judge. She modeled stewardship.

When we practice stewardship principals (wise management of time, talent, and treasure) God blesses; when we do not, judgment is pending.

Again the Israelites did evil in the LORD's sight. [They worshipped other gods.] *They abandoned the LORD and no longer served him at all. So the LORD burned with anger against Israel, and he turned them over to the Philistines and the Ammonites.... For eighteen years they oppressed all the Israelites."* (Judges 10:6-8 NLT)

Disobedience and poor stewardship come with the high price of judgment. The Israelites came to their senses, but the consequences remained. Does this sound remotely like tomorrow's headlines here in America and around the world?

Finally they cried out to the LORD for help, saying, "We have sinned against you because we have abandoned you as our God and have served the images of Baal." (Judges 10:10 NLT)

We have served the god of materialism, we have done what we felt was right in our own eyes. The consequences of poor stewardship are clear.

Yet you have abandoned me and served other gods. So I will not rescue you anymore. Go and cry out to the gods you have chosen! Let them rescue you in your hour of distress! But the Israelites pleaded with the Lord and said, "We have sinned. Punish us as you see fit, only rescue us today from our enemies." Then the Israelites put aside their foreign gods and served the LORD. And he was grieved by their misery. (Judges 10:13-16 NLT)

These passages are absolutely relevant in our current stewardship and financial arena. We have abandoned God and he has said to us, "Cry out to Wall Street and to Congress and to your banking institution and see if they can rescue you in your hour of need!"

STEWARDSHIP PRINCIPLE: Obedient Owners are rewarded; disobedient owners will be judged.

Ruth

The practice of stewardship is a generational issue. A generous heart is something that God places within a person but I believe that the practice of being generous can be both taught and caught.

No matter how godly your mother-in-law may be, do you want to spend the rest of your life with her? Tough question, but one that Ruth answered readily in this short Old Testament narrative.

The book of Ruth illustrates the impact family, faith, and relationships can make for generations to come. A true steward has a godly perspective on life that involves investing time, talent, and treasure in your family. The book of Ruth defines this unique family, generational, stewardship relationship:

"Look," Naomi said to her, "your sister-in-law has gone back to her people and to her gods. You should do the same."

But Ruth replied, "Don't ask me to leave you and turn back. Wherever you go, I will go; wherever you live, I will live. Your people will be my people, and your God will be my God. Wherever you die, I will die, and there I will be buried. May the LORD punish me severely if I allow anything but death to separate us!" (Ruth 1:15-17 NLT)

STEWARDSHIP PRINCIPLE: Practice stewardship as an immediate and extended family; pass along God's faithful provisions to this generation and the next.

1 Samuel

Stewardship is a commitment of our entire being to live out a biblical world life perspective. God called Samuel to such a lifestyle, and Samuel answered, "Speak, LORD, your servant is listening" (1 Sam. 3:9 NLT).

In chapter 1:11, Hannah makes a stewardship vow to the Lord, promising that if God would bless her with a son she would commit the lad to Jehovah. "He will be yours for his entire lifetime" (NLT). She makes good on her vow to commit Samuel's time, talent, and treasure to the Lord.

"I asked the LORD to give me this boy, and he has granted my request. Now I am giving him to the LORD, and he will belong to the LORD his whole life." (1 Sam. 1:27-28 NLT)

Have you made that stewardship/management decision with your children?

STEWARDSHIP PRINCIPLE: Commit your family, your children, all that you have to God, and he will bless your life as an Obedient Owner.

2 Samuel

This book is all about accountability. God holds David responsible for his behavior and praises him as a great leader; however, because he is a warrior king, God will not allow him to build the temple. Many stewardship references are found when unpacking the narrative in this book. David remained faithful in his stewardship practices; after a great victory where his enemies presented him with an array of gifts, he immediately committed those spoils of war to Jehovah.

King David dedicated all these gifts to the LORD, as he did with the silver and gold from the other nations he had defeated. (2 Sam. 8:11 NLT)

David sought to make an expensive purchase of Araunah's oxen to present a burnt offering to Jehovah. Araunah tried to refuse the king's money and basically said, "No big deal. You can have the oxen. No charge!" But King David refused to be a part of "cheap stewardship."

But the king replied to Araunah, "No, I insist on buying it, for I will not present burnt offerings to the LORD my God that have cost me nothing." So David paid him fifty pieces of silver for the threshing floor and the oxen. (2 Sam. 24:24 NLT)

David went on the make the sacrifice to Jehovah, one that was costly, as a measure of a faithful stewardship.

STEWARDSHIP PRINCIPLE: Be obedient and set aside an amount to give. Share generously when your capacity is small, and allow it to grow as your ability increases. Become an Obedient Owner and a sacrificial giver.

> *King David refused to be a part of cheap stewardship.*

1 Kings

Solomon was a steward of God's resources and built the temple to unite all of the children of Israel. Solomon, by not living off his father's giving but establishing his own stewardship practices, was rewarded with a gift from God: He was granted wisdom.

Solomon loved the LORD and followed all the instructions of his father, David, except that Solomon too offered sacrifices and burned incense at the local altars. (1 Kings 3:3 NLT)

God was pleased by Solomon's generous stewardship practices and blessed him by granting his humble request for wisdom.

Give me an understanding heart so that I can govern your people well and know the difference between right and wrong. For who by himself is able to govern this great people of yours?" The LORD was pleased that Solomon had asked for wisdom. (1 Kings 3:9-10 NLT)

God not only granted him wisdom but also promised him a long life for his faithfulness. The life of a steward is one of wisdom and faithfulness.

STEWARDSHIP PRINCIPLE: Obedient Owners are faithful managers of all that God has entrusted to them. He may also choose to bless them with their heart's desire (as he did for Solomon with wisdom).

2 Kings

Stewardship is generational, as is leadership. The book of 2 Kings describes some interesting leadership issues. The first describes the leadership mantle being passed from Elijah to Elisha. Leadership is the stewardship/management of the talent God has entrusted to us.

Elisha picked up Elijah's cloak, which had fallen when he was taken up. Then Elisha returned to the bank of the Jordan River. He struck the water with Elijah's cloak and cried out, "Where is the LORD, the God of Elijah?" Then the river divided, and Elisha went across. When the group of prophets from Jericho saw from a distance what happened, they exclaimed, "Elijah's spirit rests upon Elisha!" And they went to meet him and bowed to the ground before him. (2 Kings 2:13-15 NLT)

The second stewardship passage is about money that the priests had not used as God has instructed. It's an example of poor stewardship. The Levites had collected money to repair the temple (capital expenses) and instead had spent the money on their own needs (operational needs). Even the Internal Revenue Service insists that you honor the wishes of a donor by spending the money according to the donor's wishes.

So King Joash called for Jehoiada and the other priests and asked them, "Why haven't you repaired the Temple? Don't use any more money for your own needs. From now on, it must all be spent on Temple repairs." So the priests agreed not to accept any more money from the people, and they also agreed to let others take responsibility for repairing the Temple. Then Jehoiada the priest bored a hole in the lid of a large chest and set it on the right-hand side of the altar at the entrance of the Temple of the LORD. The priests guarding the entrance put all of the people's contributions into the chest. Whenever the chest became full, the court secretary and the high priest counted the money that had been brought to the LORD's Temple and put it into bags. Then they gave the money to the construction supervisors, who used it to pay the people working on the LORD's Temple ... (12:7-11 NLT).

STEWARDSHIP PRINCIPLE: A steward has integrity and transparency, and is honest in all aspects of life.

1 Chronicles

David helps the Levites get their act together and carry the ark of the covenant into Jerusalem in preparation for the building of a permanent temple in chapter 15.

Solomon is the stewardship officer/chief fundraiser for the temple.

> *"Using every resource at my command, I have gathered as much as I could for building the Temple of my God. . . . And now, because of my devotion to the Temple of my God, I am giving all of my own private treasures of gold and silver to help in the construction. This is in addition to the building materials I have already collected for his holy Temple."* (1 Chron. 29:2-3 NLT)

Solomon goes on to describe how much he will give to ensure the temple project is a success and it definitely makes him a Major Donor.

Solomon's gift of wisdom is once again defined later in the book. Here he acknowledges the God who entrusted all of those resources to manage. He clearly states that God alone is the owner and he is a mere manager of riches, the earthly kingdom. Solomon got it right. He was an Obedient Owner.

> *Yours, O Lord, is the greatness, the power, the glory, the victory, and the majesty. Everything in the heavens and on earth is yours, O Lord, and this is your kingdom. We adore you as the one who is over all things. Wealth and honor come from you alone, for you rule*

over everything. Power and might are in your hand, and at your discretion people are made great and given strength. (1 Chron. 29:11-12 NLT)

STEWARDSHIP PRINCIPLE: By practicing obedient ownership you will honor God, the owner of all, and encourage others to be Obedient Owners as well.

2 Chronicles

The heart of the steward is one of humility, one that acknowledges the Creator God who has the power to forgive the sin of misusing our resources.

A very familiar verse in this book is a verse about stewardship. Our wickedness has shown itself in the way we manage resources: money, people, possessions, children, businesses and investments, just to name a few.

Then if my people who are called by my name will humble themselves and pray and seek my face and turn from their wicked ways, I will hear from heaven and will forgive their sins and restore their land. (2 Chron. 7:14 NLT)

Hezekiah the priest was delighted to help Solomon get the temple built and ready for worship. Solomon and Hezekiah were not shy in challenging the people to be generous stewards.

In addition, he [Solomon] required the people in Jerusalem to bring a portion of their goods to the priests and Levites, so they could devote themselves fully to the Law of the LORD. The people of Israel responded immediately and generously by bringing the first of their crops and grain, new wine, olive oil, honey, and all the produce of their fields. They brought a large quantity—a tithe of all they produced. (2 Chron. 31:4-5 NLT)

Any questions about tithing and giving? Read those verses again.

STEWARDSHIP PRINCIPLE: Be a generous tither and giver. It could heal a nation—perhaps yours!

Ezra

Ezra, Haggai, and Zechariah all address the return of Israel and Judah from exile and the task of rebuilding the temple that Solomon built and the Babylonians destroyed. For seventy years they were in captivity, and this is the exciting story of their return to Jerusalem to rebuild the temple. Ezra is a narrative of second chances. God is all about the second chance. He has certainly granted me many second chances.

To rebuild, they needed to raise monies and material. They needed a capital campaign. They weren't looking for everyone to give the same amount, but they expected each person give what they could.

When they arrived at the Temple of the LORD in Jerusalem, some of the family leaders made voluntary offerings toward the rebuilding of God's Temple on its original site, and each leader gave as much as he could. The total of their gifts came to 61,000 gold coins, 6,250 pounds of silver, and 100 robes for the priests. (Ezra 2:68-69 NLT)

The campaign was successful, generosity abounded, and God was honored in this second chance campaign.

STEWARDSHIP PRINCIPLE: It is not about equal giving but equal sacrifice. Give according to your means.

Nehemiah

This whole book is about a man who was a faithful steward in spite of his circumstances. He was a slave, and his job in King Artaxerxes' palace was that of the kitchen steward. He made sure the king and queen were well fed—and were not poisoned (a method of replacing a number of kings in Old Testament times). I believe he became a close friend of the king and won his heart because of faithful service and careful management of the entire palace.

In chapter one Nehemiah acknowledged the sins of Israel that caused them to be exiled and punished. He also prayed to God that the king would grant his request to go back home to Jerusalem and rebuild the walls of the city. The only way that could happen was if Artaxerxes would grant his stewardship wish. Nehemiah needed these four requests to be granted for the campaign to be successful.

1. Time off work to travel to Judah to build the wall of his ancestors
2. A letter to insure safe travel
3. Soldiers to insure their safety
4. Workers and material to begin the project immediately upon arrival

Nehemiah's request was one of time, talent, and treasure, a unique stewardship request that was granted. Through this God performed a miracle among those captives.

Be a faithful steward regardless of your circumstance.

STEWARDSHIP PRINCIPLE: Be a faithful steward regardless of your circumstances.

Esther

Personal influence is a major part of your stewardship practice and lifestyle. Who do you have the opportunity to influence on a daily, weekly, and monthly basis? Are you using that influence to honor God with your life and to serve others? Remember the great commandment—to love the Lord your God with all your heart, soul, and mind, and to love your neighbor. Esther understood all of that as she used her influence to save her people from an almost certain holocaust.

Esther risked her own life to save her people. Mordecai asked Esther to use her influence. If the king had not acknowledged this Jewish girl's entrance into his court, she could have been killed. Mordecai says to his adopted daughter, Esther:

> *"If you keep quiet at a time like this, deliverance and relief for the Jews will arise from some other place, but you and your relatives will die. Who knows if perhaps you were made queen for just such a time as this?"* (Esther 4:14 NLT)

Has God placed you in a special position to be a heavenly manager/owner and use your time, your influence, and affluence to make a significant impact? That's the $64 question—or perhaps the $64,000 question. Live your life as an Obedient Owner.

STEWARDSHIP PRINCIPLE: Biblical stewards use their influence at the right time and in the right places, and God blesses them with the right outcome.

Job

The book of Job is a narrative of a faithful steward. Job was not only an owner but an Obedient Owner, a mere manager of the resources God had entrusted to him—wealth, family, friends, and even his health. If Job had been a disobedient owner, he might have taken his own life—as many have done during less trying economic and personal downturns. His faith and trust was in God not in materialism, not even in good health. Boils from head to toe may have been a showstopper for many.

God tested Job's life and lifestyle and he passed with flying colors. At one point Job even used his lifestyle as a steward to defend himself to his friends.

All who heard of me praised me. All who saw me spoke well of me. For I assisted the poor in their need and the orphans required help. (Job 29:11-12 NLT)

He picks up his defense again in 29:15-16:

I served as eyes for the blind and feet for the lame. I was a father to the poor and assisted strangers who needed help.

In spite of severe difficulty, Job remained a faithful steward. Oh, that we could do the same during these times of a meltdown in our global economy.

STEWARDSHIP PRINCIPLE: Be faithful to practice stewardship when times are good and when they are bad.

Psalms

The psalmists were very practical stewards who penned much about God's goodness, his greatness, and his ownership of the universe and everything in it.

The earth is the LORD's, and everything in it. The world and all its people belong to him. (Ps. 24:1 NLT)

The psalmist calls for our generosity in all circumstances of life.

Good comes to those who lend money generously and conduct their business fairly. Such people will not be overcome by evil. Those who are righteous will be long remembered. They do not fear bad news; they confidently trust the LORD to care for them. (Ps. 112:5-7 NLT)

God is sovereign in everything including our financial affairs.

Can I hear someone say, "Amen?" We need not fear our existing economic conditions because—as the psalmist says through these 150 hymns—God is sovereign in everything, including our financial affairs.

STEWARDSHIP PRINCIPLE: Generous stewards will not be overcome by evil schemes but will be blessed as they practice obedient ownership.

Proverbs

The book of wisdom is chock full of passages regarding stewardship. I believe wisdom and stewardship are terms that fit together. Every biblical steward I have met in person—and there have been many in serving over fifteen hundred clients the past thirty years—is wise, though not all to the same degree. They are astute managers. The success of foolish stewards doesn't often last very long. Those unwise stewards who mishandle their time, talent, and treasure often end up losing those resources.

If you are unsure that lack of wisdom and resources impacts the bottom line, read this: "Lazy people want much but get little, but those who work hard will prosper" (Prov. 13:4 NLT).

God is a logical being. In Proverbs the teacher points out many if/then scenarios and gives sound advice on how to live a prudent life so that good consequences may result.

I have riches and honor, as well as enduring wealth and justice.
   My gifts are better than gold, even the purest gold, my wages better than sterling silver!
   Those who love me inherit wealth. I will fill their treasuries.
(Prov. 8:18-19, 21 NLT)

Any additional questions on the vast difference between the unwise manager and the godly steward?

STEWARDSHIP PRINCIPLE: Obedient Owners are hard workers and God prospers them with a satisfied life.

Ecclesiastes

Solomon, a man of great wisdom, addressed many aspects of our lives as stewards. Chapter 3 is a unique perspective on time management in our busy world—and time management is a critical component of our lives as stewards.

If stewardship is truly everything we do after we say we believe (from the foot of the cross to the foot of the grave), then we all must discipline ourselves to redeem the time entrusted to us. They say seventy years is the benchmark for how long a person will live in the United States, and it goes by pretty quickly. My next decade is the sixth I will have lived, and I appear to be closer to the end than to the beginning. I'm challenged to use my time wisely.

> *For everything there is a season, a time for every activity under heaven.*
> *A time to be born and a time to die.*
> *A time to plant and a time to harvest.*
> *A time to kill and a time to heal. A time to tear down and a time to build up.*
> *A time to cry and a time to laugh. A time to grieve and a time to dance. (Eccl. 3:1-4 NLT)*

Ecclesiastes is often considered to have a rather gloomy message; but when you consider these verses you realize that using time wisely—whether working or resting, earning or giving—makes life meaningful. This is our call as Obedient Owners.

Stewards use their time wisely.

STEWARDSHIP PRINCIPLE: Stewards use their time wisely.

Song of Solomon

The gift of sexuality was ordained by God to be managed within the bond of holy matrimony. This glorious gift from God is to be used wisely and responsibly within a marriage, between a man and a woman as described in this book. Like any stewardship resource, marriage too needs accountability. As stewards we are held responsible to our marriage vows and our partner.

I am my lover's, and my lover is mine. (Songs 6:3a NLT)

STEWARDSHIP PRINCIPLE: God owns all of us. Even our bodies, in the context of intimacy with our spouse, are a subject of our Obedient Ownership.

Isaiah

The ultimate steward (the Christ child) came to earth to save his people from their sin. Isaiah is a book of great hope, promising the hope of redemption. It lays out the faith, hope, practice, and purpose of the biblical steward. God created us to be generous people.

Share your food with the hungry,
and give shelter to the homeless.
Give clothes to those who need them,
and do not hide from relatives who need your help.
Then your salvation will come like the dawn,
and your wounds will quickly heal.
Your godliness will lead you forward,
and the glory of the LORD will protect you from behind.
(Isa. 58:7-8 NLT)

If you are practicing biblical stewardship, do you know who's got your back? Jehovah, the God of this Universe! That alone should help us be generous with our time, talent, and treasure, practicing obedient ownership.

STEWARDSHIP PRINCIPLE: We cannot outgive God, and he's got our back.

Jeremiah

God is the ultimate steward. He gives watchful care over all creation. In the midst of faithless living, poor stewardship, and broken covenants, God's wrath was being poured out on Israel. He reminds his people that he is their steward, their manager, their overseer. He modeled stewardship for the whole world from the beginning and will do so until the end.

"O Sovereign LORD! You made the heavens and earth by your strong hand and powerful arm. Nothing is too hard for you! You show unfailing love to thousands, but you also bring the consequences of one generation's sin upon the next. You are the great and powerful God, the LORD of Heaven's Armies. You have all wisdom and do great and mighty miracles. You see the conduct of all people, and you give them what they deserve. You performed miraculous signs and wonders in the land of Egypt—things still remembered to this day! And you have continued to do great miracles in Israel and all around the world. You have made your name famous to this day." (Jer. 32:17-20 NLT)

STEWARDSHIP PRINCIPLE: God is aware of my conduct as a steward and will reward my faithfulness.

Lamentations

To lament is to express deep grief, often audibly. Out of sorrow comes faith. The life of the steward is one of deep faith. When we experience those times of sorrow, setback, and loss, God reminds us that he is there for us. He helps us manage and steward our way through those times.

The faithful love of the LORD never ends! His mercies never cease. Great is his faithfulness; his mercies begin afresh each morning. (Lam. 3:22-23 NLT)

God commands the steward to be faithful and put our hope, trust, and future in him, regardless of the circumstances. Lament, but keep a steward's perspective.

STEWARDSHIP PRINCIPLE: Even during times of sorrow and grief acknowledge God's sovereignty and stewardship plan for our lives.

Ezekiel

This book is all about rebirth; God breathes life into dead bones and they walk again (Eze. 37). God reminded the people of the plan, purpose, and blessing of offering sacrifices (Eze. 43:18-27). In the Old Testament, stewards kept the levitical law by following—or at least attempting to follow—every jot and tittle through their Jewish tradition and the prophet.

On the eighth day, and on each day afterward, the priests will sacrifice on the altar the burnt offerings and peace offerings of the people. Then I will accept you. I, the Sovereign LORD, have spoken! (Eze. 43:27 NLT)

STEWARDSHIP PRINCIPLE: God promises to accept and honor our sacrifice as stewards.

Daniel

Daniel was managing his life as an Obedient Owner. He wanted to please God even as a slave in Babylon. He would not defile his body or his mind with the king's food or drink. Because of his courage and faith as a steward in a foreign land God blessed him above all others.

Daniel was an obedient owner

Daniel soon proved himself more capable than all the other administrators and high officers. Because of Daniel's great ability, the king made plans to place him over the entire empire. Then the other administrators and high officers began searching for some fault in the way Daniel was handling government affairs, but they couldn't find anything to criticize or condemn. He was faithful, always responsible, and completely trustworthy. (Dan. 6:3-4 NLT)

Daniel could stand before God and hear him say, "Well done, you good and faithful steward!"

STEWARDSHIP PRINCIPLE: Be a faithful steward even in the trials and God will bless and use you.

Hosea

The prophet Hosea wrote about God's incredible love. We are empowered as stewards by that unchanging love. God loves Israel in spite of years of unfaithful stewardship. To illustrate that truth, Hosea is commanded to marry an unfaithful bride.

When the LORD first began speaking to Israel through Hosea, he said to him, "Go and marry a prostitute, so that some of her children will be conceived in prostitution. This will illustrate how Israel has acted like a prostitute by turning against the LORD and worshiping other gods." So Hosea married Gomer. (Hos. 1:2-3a NLT)

To live a life of faith totally sold out to God's principals of stewardship is not easy because we all have many opportunities to be disobedient owners. To love things and money more than we love people and God, is not the right stewardship practice. God's radical love for us is humbling. We show our love to him by being obedient stewards.

STEWARDSHIP PRINCIPLE: Be faithful in all things and be an Obedient Owner.

Joel

The minor prophets' perspective on stewardship often involved pending judgment because of the unfaithful practices, traditions, and habits of God's chosen people. Joel was reading the Israelites' sentence to encourage them to repent. Joel mirrored that theme as he invited Israel to pass along to present and future generations the consequences of God's judgment because of their sin, their turning away from his ways.

Tell your children about it in the years to come, and let your children tell their children. Pass the story down from generation to generation. (Joel 1:3 NLT)

In essence Joel was saying, "Live your life as a faithful steward, or judgment will come. God has the final say but if they will repent and turn their life and practices around there is hope."

A millennial passage makes this promise to Israel:

I will give back what you have lost.... Then you will know that I am among my people Israel, that I am the LORD your God.... I will pour out my Spirit upon all people. Your sons and daughters will prophesy. Your old men will dream dreams, and your young men will see visions. (Joel 2:25-28 NLT)

Their faith and God's promise will once again restore them as a part of God's vision. Part of God's vision for our generation is that we will live our lives as faithful stewards.

STEWARDSHIP PRINCIPLE: God wants us to repent and become faithful kingdom managers, Obedient Owners.

Amos

Our charge as a biblical steward is to live our lives as generous people who are upright, just, and holy. Israel fell way short of that mandate and was judged harshly many times. If stewardship is not practiced, if people do not become mature in this area, the results are personal, cultural, and spiritual bankruptcy—not to mention God's judgment!

All nine chapters of Amos deal with Israel the unfaithful steward. God reveals ongoing displeasure with their vain attempts at righteousness and stewardship. Amos quotes God as saying:

> *I will not accept your burnt offerings and grain offerings. I won't even notice all your choice peace offerings. Away with your noisy hymns of praise! I will not listen to the music of your harps. Instead, I want to see a mighty flood of justice, an endless river of righteous living.* (Amos 5:22-24 NLT)

I believe this is exactly what God wants of us today as well: a river of righteous living, careful and prayerful practice of stewardship; in doing so we will impact our world with the

If stewardship is not practiced, the results are personal, cultural, and spiritual bankruptcy.

power of God's love, mercy, and grace. Amos prophesied when Judah and Israel were experiencing prosperity. Since "all was well" in the land they very likely marginalized God. Sounds a bit like our situation today. Wall Street, Forbes, and Money Magazine all have more impact on our lifestyles than God's word does.

STEWARDSHIP PRINCIPLE: A biblical steward promotes and practices righteousness, holiness, and justice in good economic times as well as in the lean times.

Obadiah

"The Day of the LORD is near...." Oh, that the Church of Jesus Christ around the world and especially in our western culture would realize we need to be Obedient Owners, managers and stewards of God resources. Obadiah reminds us that the past, the present, and the future are not in our hands but in the hands of the Almighty.

The day is near when I, the Lord, will judge all godless nations! As you have done to Israel, so it will be done to you. All your evil deeds will fall back on your own heads. (Obadiah 1:15 NLT)

Responsible stewards live their lives according to God's plan and purpose and they practice righteous living and giving.

STEWARDSHIP PRINCIPLE: Stewards live responsible lives and take responsibility for their actions.

Jonah

One message in the book of Jonah is that of ultimately being a "faithful steward," albeit with the help of some divine coaxing. During a high seas escape attempt, Jonah was tossed overboard and swallowed by a great fish, which God used to redirect him back toward Nineveh. After initially being disobedient, Jonah turned back to minister where God wanted him.

Jonah confessed his sin and offered his faithful sacrifice and recommitment as an Obedient Owner.

As my life was slipping away, I remembered the LORD. And my earnest prayer went out to you in your holy Temple. Those who worship false gods turn their backs on all God's mercies. But I will offer sacrifices to you with songs of praise, and I will fulfill all my vows. For my salvation comes from the LORD alone. (Jonah 2:7-9 NLT)

STEWARDSHIP PRINCIPLE: A steward understands it is our merciful God who gives us all things including our safety and our salvation.

Micah

This book by the prophet Micah is a classic narrative of God's displeasure with the Samarians and those living in Jerusalem for being unwise and unfaithful stewards. Once again Jehovah was ready to judge Israel for its transgressions.

Attention! Let all the people of the world listen!
  Let the earth and everything in it hear.
The Sovereign Lord is making accusations against you;
  the Lord speaks from his holy Temple.
Look! The Lord is coming!
  He leaves his throne in heaven
  and tramples the heights of the earth. (Micah 1:2-3 NLT)

The prophet is reminding them again that Jehovah is the ultimate owner of all they have or ever will have, and he is coming to judge them because of their misused lives and misguided lifestyles.

He closes the book with two key statements about the promise of God's unfailing love and His mercy for Israel and for us: "You do not stay angry forever but delight to show mercy." (Micah 7:18b NIV). "You will show us your faithfulness and unfailing love as you promised to our ancestors Abraham and Jacob long ago." (Micah 7:20a NLT).

STEWARDSHIP PRINCIPLE: A steward models God's love and shows mercy to all of his creation and creatures.

Nahum

This prophet's message is to Nineveh and to the nation of Judah. Nahum associates God's anger with their faithless living and poor stewardship. He reminds them of God's control of all of his creation.

The LORD is a jealous God, filled with vengeance and rage ... The LORD is slow to get angry, but his power is great .... At his command the oceans dry up, and the rivers disappear. The lush pastures of Bashan and Carmel fade, and the green forests of Lebanon wither. In his presence the mountains quake, and the hills melt away; the earth trembles, and its people are destroyed. (Nahum 1:2-5 NLT)

Defining his power as a Ruler over all, Jehovah clearly establishes himself as the owner. He tells Judah that they can either serve and be faith-

God's anger was due to their faithless living and poor stewardship.

ful stewards or reap the impending judgment for the misuse of God's resources. Yet, as we have observed every time, God also expresses his love, and promises to bless Judah if they will put their trust in him.

The LORD is good, a strong refuge when trouble comes.
He is close to those who trust in him. (Nahum 1:7 NLT)

STEWARDSHIP PRINCIPLE: A steward trusts God in everything because he is our strong refuge.

Habakkuk

Most of the minor prophets spoke to the people on God's behalf. Habakkuk was unique in that he spoke to God on behalf of the people. What he asked God is a fair stewardship question: "Hey, God, why do the evil prosper? Why do dishonest businessmen get richer? Why do the guys on Wall Street in their greed and power forget us little guys on Main Street?"

Must I forever see these evil deeds? Why must I watch all this misery? Wherever I look, I see destruction and violence. I am surrounded by people who love to argue and fight. The law has become paralyzed, and there is no justice in the courts. The wicked far outnumber the righteous, so that justice has become perverted. (Hab. 1:3-4 NLT)

Habakkuk is the stewardship representative for the people. He was pleading their case before God.

Chapter 2 is full of woe-to-you warnings—reminders that God will bring the wicked down, but honor those who trust in him. My mom used to say, "every dog has his day," which is true of sinners and the unrighteous and non-stewards. But the righteous steward will prevail.

Chapter 3 is a pleading prayer by Habakkuk showing God and the people he understands the need for them to return to a lifestyle of a steward. He closes his prophecy with hope.

Yet I will rejoice in the LORD! I will be joyful in the God of my salvation! The Sovereign LORD is my strength! (Hab. 3:18-19a NLT)

He gives a statement of stewardship: "All I have and all that I am comes from the LORD."

STEWARDSHIP PRINCIPLE: The unjust steward will be judged; be a wise and faithful steward, an Obedient Owner.

Zephaniah

Zephaniah shares his stewardship perspective, a unique balance between judgment and salvation, between God's anger and his compassion. The prophet does not mess around but gets right to the judgment of those unfaithful stewards. They have mismanaged their time, their talents, and their treasure.

"I will sweep away everything from the face of the earth," says the LORD. (Zeph. 1:2 NLT)

And then he spends time speaking on God's behalf regarding those on the indicted/guilty list. He promises judgment on men, animals, birds, fish, those who worship Baal, those who worship Molech, liars, cheaters, the wealthy, the poor, even on the complacent. Oh, by the way he reminds them of another great stewardship lesson: God will not be bought off with their wealth.

Your silver and gold will not save you on that day of the LORD's anger. For the whole land will be devoured by the fire of his jealousy. He will make a terrifying end of all the people on the earth. (Zeph. 1:18 NLT)

Can I hear someone make a comparison to our world, to our nation, to our state of affairs in 2011 and beyond?

Once again, I hope by now you are not tired of God's incredible promises to faithful stewards.

On that day I will gather you together and bring you home again. I will give you a good name, a name of distinction, among all the nations of the earth, as I restore your fortunes before their very eyes. I, the LORD, have spoken! (Zeph. 3:20 NLT)

STEWARDSHIP PRINCIPLE: If we are Obedient Owners, God will exalt us among all the peoples of the earth.

Haggai

If you cheated and read this chapter first, go back and read chapters one through eight. We as people, we as stewards, will not be blessed until we faithfully live our lives according to his plan and purpose for us. We are to be Obedient Owners of the resources that have been entrusted to us to be reallocated for his glory!

STEWARDSHIP PRINCIPLE: Forget the unfaithful past; seek to become a faithful steward today and you will become God's beautiful "Signet Ring."

Zechariah

A parallel book to Haggai, Zechariah speaks of the return of the captives from Babylon and of the need to rebuild the temple. God was so angry with their lifestyles he would not even hear their prayers. He promised to make their land a desert and to judge them if they did not get their act together. This is a prophetic book and promises to restore Israel as a great nation.

We have seen before that God is slow to execute his wrath, but assures the Jews and us he will have the final word. Everything is his, and he will have a say in its use and allocation. He promises to restore Israel and Judah, and to destroy all of their enemies. With all of these promises of judgment and restoration is an admonition he shares with the children of Israel, strategically placed in the middle of the book:

> *This is what the* Lord *of Heaven's Armies says: Judge fairly, and show mercy and kindness to one another. Do not oppress widows, orphans, foreigners, and the poor. And do not scheme against each other.* (Zech. 7:9-10 NLT)

Do you want a stewardship plan for your life? It's laid out for you in the verse above: show kindness and mercy, do nothing to harm each other, become a servant, be fair and honest in every experience of life. In doing so, you will model God's love for this world. That's obedient ownership!

STEWARDSHIP PRINCIPLE: Actions speak louder than words. Let the way you treat others reveal your stewardship plan.

Malachi

This unique narrative involves the prophet confronting the people about their complacency—their indifference to God and his commands. Lifestyle is such a tough issue for all biblical stewards to address. How shall we live in light of the needs of our world and God's command to meet those needs?

God is straightforward.

> *I am the* Lord, *and I do not change. That is why you descendants of Jacob are not already completely destroyed. Ever since the days of your ancestors, you have scorned my decrees and failed to obey them. Now return to me, and I will return to you," says the* Lord *of Heaven's Army. But you ask, "How can we return when we have*

never gone away?" Should people cheat God? Yet you have cheated me! But you ask, "What do you mean? When did we ever cheat you?" You have cheated me of the tithes and offerings due to me. (Mal. 3:6-8 NLT)

How do we rob God? How do we cheat God? Are we strong enough to mug God, to beat him up and rob him? Of course not. We have become embezzlers. We have taken our tithes and of-

We have been embezzlers and robbed God.

ferings and have spent them on ourselves, on our debt, on our nice houses and new cars. We have taken money God commanded us to give, and have embezzled it to service our lifestyles. Stewards don't steal from God!

STEWARDSHIP PRINCIPLE: Stewards don't embezzle from God; they give, first and foremost.

Conclusion

Some of you will not agree with my interpretation of select passages in my Old Testament overview on stewardship. I have broadened the view of stewardship to encompass lifestyle issues of our body, our mind, our heart, our thoughts, our practices—how we invest our time, our talent, and our treasure. Each defines us as a biblical steward or a wannabe.

C. I. Scofield said it well. "Stewardship cannot be faked, our checkbook defines our stewardship." He also said, "Don't show me that tattered and worn pages of a man's Bible, show me a man's checkbook and therein lie his priorities."[24]

But we all know stewardship is more than our money; it's all we are and all we hope to become. It's a life lived in the light of God's

Word and his promise to love us and prepare an eternal home for us in glory.

> We were created to praise, to reverence and to serve God. And everything on the face of the earth was created for our sake, to help us achieve the goal for which we were created.[25]

---

[24] Sermon Notes, Trinitarian Congregational Church, East Northfield, MA, 1895.

[25] Ignatius of Loyola, 1491-1556.

10

The New Testament Perspective

*"Tell those rich in the world's wealth to quit
being so full of themselves and so obsessed with
money, which is here today and gone tomorrow.
Tell them to go after God, who piles on all the
riches we could ever manage—to do good, to
be rich in helping others, to be extravagantly
generous. If they do that, they'll build a treasury
that will last, gaining life that is truly life."*
(1 Timothy 6:17-19 The Message)

*"Pray for a good harvest . . . but keep on
hoeing!"* — Sign along a rural road

We were able to shed some stewardship light on the thirty-nine
books of the Old Testament; how about the twenty-seven
books of the New Testament? After all, we Christians spend the ma-

jority of our time teaching, preaching, and studying the New Testament, not the Old. The New Testament even sounds more relevant by its very title; after all, it is *new*! We tend to live our lives in the grace and knowledge of the New Testament supported by the redemptive and stewardship narratives from the Old Testament. Remember, the Bible is a comprehensive study of the lives of real people and principles of stewardship. All of our lives as Christians are about conducting ourselves as wise managers of his resources.

Now we get to look at the stewardship perspectives of folks who hung around with Jesus, famous authors like Dr. Luke (a family practitioner) and Matthew (a tax collector and financial analyst). Peter, the small business owner of "Pete's Fisheries," wades in with a few books. James, the brother of Jesus, sheds some light (they lived together in Nazareth) on these issues. John the Beloved dives in with some unique stewardship views. The major author of the New Testament was Saul of Tarsus—known by his Christian name, Paul—a converted Roman citizen who was also a first-century terrorist; this apostle puts his spin on stewardship, New Testament style.

These twenty-seven books detail the life of Jesus, the redemption story, and the history of the first-century church, providing lots of great theology and doctrine, as well as defining how we should live as Christians. Can I hear someone say, "That's stewardship!"

Here we go on a fact-finding mission to discover a stewardship perspective in each of these canonized holy books. Once again, I will identify a stewardship principle in each of the twenty-seven books.

Matthew's Gospel

The converted tax collector for the Roman government (a first-century IRS agent) had a lot to say about stewardship, life, and money. He begins in chapter 6 defining how to give with a pure heart.

My stewardship mantra—a tune I have been singing to boards, trustees, and staff members for nearly thirty years—appears in this book.

Don't store up treasures here on earth, where moths eat them and rust destroys them, and where thieves break in and steal. Store your treasures in heaven, where moths and rust cannot destroy, and thieves do not break in and steal. Wherever your treasure is, there the desires of your heart will also be. (Matt. 6:19-21 NLT)

Do you want the heart, prayers, focus, and mind of your staff, board, and key donors? Get them to commit to regular donations. Matthew did not say if your time is there your heart will be also. He did not say if your talent is there, your heart will be there also. He clearly says where your treasure is, your heart will be there also. The heart and the checkbook are connected.

He concludes the book with perhaps one of the richest stewardship chapters in the New Testament, which speaks about the wise stewards who managed the resources of the master. Those who greatly increased the investment were awarded with more. The unwise steward who buried the treasure lost it completely for his lack of wise management.

After discussing how the shepherd separates the sheep from the goats, Matthew closes with these incredible thoughts about casting out the unfaithful, stingy, embezzling steward because he did not give when he had the opportunity.

Then the King will turn to those on the left and say, "Away with you, you cursed ones, into the eternal fire prepared for the devil and his demons. For I was hungry, and you didn't feed me. I was thirsty, and you didn't give me a drink. I was a stranger, and you didn't invite me into your home. I was naked, and you didn't give me clothing. I was sick and in prison, and you didn't visit me."

Then they will reply, "Lord, when did we ever see you hungry or thirsty or a stranger or naked or sick or in prison, and not help you?"

And he will answer, "I tell you the truth, when you refused to help the least of these my brothers and sisters, you were refusing to help me." (Matt. 25:41-46 NLT)

Want to be a faithful steward? Look for ways to impact people who need help. Do ministry with your money.

STEWARDSHIP PRINCIPLE: Your checkbook and your heart are connected. A godly steward will naturally want to give to people and organizations that touch the heart.

Want to be a faithful steward … look for ways to help people.

Mark's Gospel

Mark's gospel (the shortest of the four) is a fast-paced narrative. Like all good storytellers, Mark selected his material carefully. He fleshed out the life and times of Jesus and the people he touched; some of these events were told only by Mark. A narrative in the life and times of Jesus that Mark shares involved a large group of people who gathered near the Sea of Galilee to hear him speak. A young boy whose mother had sent him to hear the master had sent along a small lunch of five small loaves of bread and two small fish. The disciples looked around the crowd and realized the only food for these 5,000+ listeners was this lad's lunch. A stewardship miracle was in the offing.

The disciples wanted to send the crowd away to fend for themselves. Perhaps it was Judas who answered Jesus after Jesus said, "You feed them."

"With what?" they asked. "We'd have to work for months to earn enough money to buy food for all these people!" "How much bread do you have?" he asked. "Go and find out." They came back and reported, "We have five loaves of bread and two fish." (Mark 6:37-38 NLT)

Jesus' response is nothing short of miraculous:

Jesus took the five loaves and two fish, looked up toward heaven, and blessed them. Then, breaking the loaves into pieces, he kept giving the bread to the disciples so they could distribute it to the people. He also divided the fish for everyone to share. They all ate as much as they wanted, and afterward, the disciples picked up twelve baskets of leftover bread and fish. (6:41-43 NLT)

The boy gave all that he had and Jesus performed a stewardship miracle and everyone ate and they even had leftovers. In God's economy, every gift given from the heart performs miracles in the heart of the giver and in the heart of the receiver—in this instance in the stomachs of the followers.

> *In God's economy, every gift given from the heart performs miracles.*

STEWARDSHIP PRINCIPLE: Give generously from what you have. Don't worry about what you don't have. Give willingly and expect God to bless your offering for his honor and glory.

Luke's Gospel

Luke, who traveled with Jesus, perhaps might have called his gospel *A Doctor's Perspective on Ministry, Medicine, and Money.* He defines Jesus mission and ministry here on earth to be "to seek and to save the lost" (19:10). But the good doctor also spends time writing about all the miracles Jesus performed and talking about stewardship. This book is chock full of stewardship narratives.

Chapter 12 is worthy of an in-depth study.

> *Then he said, "Beware! Guard against every kind of greed. Life is not measured by how much you own." (Luke 12:15 NLT)*

Luke uses this introduction as a springboard to share the parable of the rich fool who tears down big barns to build even bigger ones.

> *But God said to him, "You fool! You will die this very night. Then who will get everything you worked for?" Yes, a person is a fool to*

store up earthly wealth but not have a rich relationship with God. (Luke 12:20-21 NLT)

Chapters 14, 16, and 19 are also rich with stewardship teachings. Chapter 14 speaks of careful and prayerful planning so a steward does not embarrass himself in front of his neighbors and the world. Be a strategic steward; don't lay out big plans that you cannot finish!

Chapter 16 says, "No one can serve two masters. For you will hate one and love the other; you will be devoted to one and despise the other. You cannot serve both God and money" (Luke 16:13 NLT).

You cannot serve God and money.

Chapter 19 shares the parable of the ten minas; it speaks of the blessings bestowed upon the faithful steward and the loss that will be incurred by the unfaithful steward. This unique gospel by Dr. Luke addresses how we use our time, our talent, and our treasure to please and glorify God.

STEWARDSHIP PRINCIPLE: Be a careful planner; invest wisely so more money can be invested in ministry. Whether you are rich or poor, be content and faithful with what you have been entrusted to manage.

John's Gospel

John wrote to both Jews and Gentiles, confirming that Jesus is the promised Messiah and Son of God. A number of stewardship concepts and narratives can be found in these 21 chapters. Chapter 6 is a synoptic retelling of the story of the young boy and his lunch and the feeding of the multitudes. John tells us it was Andrew who found the lad and asked him to share his lunch.

Stewardship is all about obedience. Do we choose to obey God's commands to be faithful and generous?

Jesus said to the people who believed in him, "You are truly my disciples if you remain faithful to my teachings. And you will know the truth, and the truth will set you free." (John 8:31-32 NLT)

What if I rephrased verse 31 to read, "You are truly my stewards if you keep obeying my teachings." Does that stretch you? Remember, my goal for me and for you is for us to grow and mature in our faith and become Obedient Owners.

In chapter 13 Jesus, the ultimate steward, showed his heart by washing the feet of the disciples. Want to be a faithful steward? Become a servant with your time, talent, and treasure.

STEWARDSHIP PRINCIPLE: We can honor our Messiah, the Son of God, by being servants, as he was, and by obeying his teachings, as they will set us free to live life as a steward.

Acts

The book of Acts is a historical account of the establishment and growth of the early church following the resurrection of Jesus. In establishing those early churches there were many stewardship stories.

I wonder if the church in the twenty-first century could function under this scenario:

All the believers devoted themselves to the apostles' teaching, and to fellowship, and to sharing in meals (including the Lord's Supper), and to prayer.

A deep sense of awe came over them all, and the apostles

performed many miraculous signs and wonders. And all the believers met together in one place and shared everything they had. They sold their property and possessions and shared the money with those in need. They worshiped together at the Temple each day, met in homes for the Lord's Supper, and shared their meals with great joy and generosity. (Acts 2:42-46 NLT)

There is the job description for your church, your small group ministry, and yourself individually.

Chapter 5 tells us how not to practice your stewardship. Ananias and Sapphira were killed, not for holding back a part of their gift, but for lying about it! Clearly this was an unfortunate move by disobedient owners, managing according to their own wishes and not those of God, the true owner. Integrity is a key part of the life of a steward. Acts 20:35 says: "It is more blessed to give than to receive."

STEWARDSHIP PRINCIPLE: Look to meet needs in your local church and local ministries, places where you can be a firsthand steward. Be honest and upfront about the giving; don't say you'll give a gift and then lie about the amount.

It is more blessed to give ....

Romans

This book shares the reality of God's judgment and his saving mercy in the gospel of Christ. Sinful behavior (like poor stewardship) is judged on the cross, and the saving mercy of God is revealed by Jesus, the ultimate steward, through his ultimate sacrifice.

Stewardship is a lifelong commitment. Paul addresses that issue in these verses clearly defining the job description of the steward:

And so, dear brothers and sisters, I plead with you to give your bodies to God because of all he has done for you. Let them be a living and holy sacrifice—the kind he will find acceptable. This is truly the way to worship him. Don't copy the behavior and customs of this world, but let God transform you into a new person by changing the way you think. Then you will learn to know God's will for you, which is good and pleasing and perfect. (Rom. 12:1-2 NLT)

As stewards, our lifestyle should shout to the world that we are a child of God. We are not conformed to this world but transformed by the power of God that is at work in our lives.

How about the stewardship, the management, the investment of our time and talent in our stewardship quest?

> *Our lifestyle should shout to the world that we are a child of God.*

In his grace, God has given us different gifts for doing certain things well. So if God has given you the ability to prophesy, speak out with as much faith as God has given you. If your gift is serving others, serve them well. If you are a teacher, teach well. If your gift is to encourage others, be encouraging. If it is giving, give generously. If God has given you leadership ability, take the responsibility seriously. And if you have a gift for showing kindness to others, do it gladly. Don't just pretend to love others. Really love them. Hate what is wrong. Hold tightly to what is good. Love each other with genuine affection, and take delight in honoring each other. Never be lazy, but work hard and serve the Lord enthusiastically. (Rom. 12:6-11 NLT)

Hear the good word of stewardship:

When God's people are in need, be ready to help them. Always be eager to practice hospitality. (Rom. 12:13 NLT)

The golden rule of the steward is in this book:

Give to everyone what you owe them: Pay your taxes and government fees to those who collect them, and give respect and honor to those who are in authority. Owe nothing to anyone—except for your obligation to love one another. If you love your neighbor, you will fulfill the requirements of God's law. (Rom. 13:7-8 NLT)

This book is so rich in stewardship narratives I wish I could keep going. Paul the apostle "shucked it down to the cob"—bringing us straight to the heart of the issue. The lives of Obedient Owners reflect the owner, God the Father and his son the Lord Jesus.

STEWARDSHIP PRINCIPLE: Give God and your neighbors your very best. As you serve him, you will also serve those around you. Pay your taxes on time; pay your workers and your debts. Be hospitable.

1 Corinthians

Paul wanted these wealthy believers to work together and stop flaunting their possessions as it was impacting those weak in the faith and unbelievers. If there was a potential for bad stewardship practices, the church at Corinth was the poster child.

Paul does not talk about their money in chapter 12 but about their gifts of time and talent, and how they invest them in the body of Christ. He reminds them these gifts are also from the Lord.

There are different kinds of spiritual gifts, but the same Spirit is the source of them all. There are different kinds of service, but we serve the same Lord. God works in different ways, but it is the same God who does the work in all of us. A spiritual gift is given to each of us so we can help each other. (1 Cor. 12:4-7 NLT)

The Holy Spirit distributes these gifts among us stewards to be used to build up the church and Christian organizations, to bring in nonbelievers, and to help ministries get funded.

Paul closes the book with another brief reminder about giving.

Now regarding your question about the money being collected for God's people in Jerusalem. You should follow the same procedure I gave to the churches in Galatia. On the first day of each week, you should each put aside a portion of the money you have earned. Don't wait until I get there and then try to collect it all at once. (1 Cor. 16:1-2 NLT)

If you still have questions on tithing and giving, read 1 Corinthians 16:1-2 once again carefully.

STEWARDSHIP PRINCIPLE: Use every gift at your disposal to build up the church. Help people; be generous and systematic in your giving. Your giving should be reflective of your ability and capacity; it is not about equal giving but about equal sacrifice.

2 Corinthians

The apostle runs a fundraising campaign for the persecuted believers in Jerusalem in this second letter to the Corinthian believers. He says to the church members in Corinth:

You have money and your fellow believers in Jerusalem have needs. I want you to help them by sending them a generous gift to buy food as they were being starved and persecuted by the Roman Government. (Pat's perceived paraphrase of Paul's speech to the Corinthians)

Chapter 8 and 9 are two great hallmarks in the stewardship writings and teachings of Paul. This book was written while Paul was in Macedonia. He must have read the parts of the letter to the Macedonian believers and shared with them the needs of the Jerusalem believers because as he was making a plea for funds from the Corinthians, the Macedonians got very excited about giving as well. Here was Paul's dilemma: the Corinthians were "filthy rich" but the Macedonians were "dirt poor." He did not even ask the Macedonians to help because of their poverty, but they begged him to let them help.

Now I want you to know, dear brothers and sisters, what God in his kindness has done through the churches in Macedonia. They are being tested by many troubles, and they are very poor. But they are also filled with abundant joy, which has overflowed in rich generosity. For I can testify that they gave not only what they could afford, but far more. And they did it of their own free will. They begged us again and again for the privilege of sharing in the gift for the believers in Jerusalem. They even did more than we had hoped, for their first action was to give themselves to the Lord and to us, just as God wanted them to do. (2 Cor. 8:1-5 NLT)

Paul uses the poverty of the Macedonians to once again challenge the wealthy.

Paul uses the poverty of the Macedonians to once again challenge the wealthy Corinthians.

Since you excel in so many ways—in your faith, your gifted speakers, your knowledge, your enthusiasm, and your love from us—I want you to excel also in this gracious act of giving. I am not commanding you to do this. But I am testing how genuine your love is by comparing it with the eagerness of the other churches. You know the generous grace of our Lord Jesus Christ. Though he was rich, yet for your sakes he became poor, so that by his poverty he could make you rich. (2 Cor. 8:7-9 NLT)

Is it a goal for your life to excel in the grace of giving? Were you a generous giver before you were making big bucks? Did you write a check to your church or favorite ministry back then when you weren't sure where it was coming from? That is when we know we are growing in the grace of giving. Your giving is first and foremost in your personal life. Obedient Ownership is the heart felt practice of true biblical stewards.

STEWARDSHIP PRINCIPLE: Rich or poor, we need to be generous givers. Stewards dedicate their time, talent, and treasure to the Lord. He blesses those who put their trust in him.

Galatians

The author of this book was all about New Testament grace. He states that justification is by faith, not by works or our vain attempts to fulfill the law.

We are not bound by the law but by grace, hence it makes us all equal in Christ. No one is higher or lower; no one is richer or poorer. (Gal. 2:16 McLaughlin paraphrased)

He writes of his friends James, Peter, and John (who were still alive when he wrote this epistle) and how they encouraged him to be generous:

> *Their only suggestion was that we keep on helping the poor* ....
> (Gal. 2:10a NLT)

Paul indicated he would heed their call of stewardship, and did so. We are all stewards set on this journey to wisely manage resources and put them to work in God's kingdom.

> *And now that the way of faith has come, we no longer need the law as our guardian. For you are all children of God through faith in Christ Jesus. And all who have been united with Christ in baptism have put on Christ, like putting on new clothes. There is no longer Jew or Gentile, slave or free, male and female. For you are all one in Christ Jesus.* (Gal. 3:25-28 NLT)

We are all stewards on this journey.

The fifth chapter speaks of the fruit of the spirit. Are these not qualities of a biblical steward?

> *Love, joy, peace, patience, kindness, goodness, faithfulness, gentleness, self-control; against such there is no law. And those who belong to Christ Jesus [as a steward] have crucified the flesh with its passions and desires.* (Gal. 5:22-23 ESV)

STEWARDSHIP PRINCIPLE: The tithe—10% of our gross income—was an attempt to fulfill the law. The New Testament calls us to go beyond what the law demands, to make giving a lifestyle; the tithe is a great place to start but not the place to stop as we grow and mature as stewards.

Ephesians

Paul reminded the church at Ephesus to live their lives as a fitting tribute to the work of Christ on the cross—faith through grace.

Paul's prayer in chapter 3 is an example of what a steward ought to be. After all, if our lives are rooted and grounded in love we should be able to apply that to our everyday world. Pray the steward's prayer:

> *Then Christ will make his home in your hearts as you trust in him. Your roots will grow down into God's love and keep you strong. And may you have the power to understand, as all God's people should, how wide, how long, how high, and how deep his love is. May you experience the love of Christ, though it is too great to understand fully. Then you will be made complete with all the fullness of life and power that comes from God. Now all glory to God, who is able, through his mighty power at work within us, to accomplish infinitely more than we might ask or think.* (Eph. 3:17-20 NLT)

The life of the steward is one of great accomplishment, because our life is reflective of God's plan and purpose for our time, talent, and treasure.

STEWARDSHIP PRINCIPLE: As our love for God and his work and his people deepens, our commitment to living out biblical principles of stewardship will also deepen and allow us to accomplish more than we could imagine.

Philippians

"I can't get no satisfaction. Though I try and I try and I try, I can't get no satisfaction." These were the lyrics of a 60's tune by the Rolling Stones. I think it is a mantra, a creed of greed, that no matter what I have, I want more. A trait of an Obedient Owner is to be satisfied and to live within one's means. Perhaps many of us could or should live below our means. It would allow us the freedom to be more generous.

Paul encourages the church at Philippi to be genuine in their faith as evidenced by their service to God and to each other. Paul lived by whatever means God provided.

Obedient owners are satisfied and live within their means.

I know how to live on almost nothing or with everything. I have learned the secret of living in every situation, whether it is with a full stomach or empty, with plenty or little. (Phil. 4:12 NLT)

And this same God who takes care of me will supply all your needs from his glorious riches, which have been given to us in Christ Jesus. (Phil. 4:19 NLT)

If we are faithful and in line with his will, God will take care of our needs. No guarantees of getting what we want, but there is a promise to meet our needs.

STEWARDSHIP PRINCIPLE: God will take care of you; he will provide for your every need. Be content and satisfied with your present lot in life and work hard as unto the Lord. God has glorious riches for you to manage as an Obedient Owner.

Colossians

Paul's theme in Colossians is that Christ (the Steward) is Lord over all creation, all that he and his Father created.

For by him all things were created, in heaven and on earth, visible and invisible, whether thrones or dominions or rulers or authorities—all things were created through him and for him. And he is before all things, and in him all things hold together. (Col. 1:16-17a ESV)

Any questions of Christ being the Steward of the World are answered in this passage, "in him all things hold together."

The book continues by talking about the stewardship of our relationships. Stewards love, forgive and in word and deed, give thanks because they understand all things are gifts from God (Col. 3:1-17).

How about marriage and the family? We should certainly love, nurture, and manage (steward) those relationships carefully and prayerfully.

Wives, submit to your husbands, as is fitting for those who belong to the Lord. Husbands, love your wives and never treat them harshly. Children, always obey your parents, for this pleases the Lord. Fathers, do not aggravate your children, or they will become discouraged. (Col. 3:18-21 NLT)

Chapter 4 addresses the lifestyle issue of how we manage our employees because God will manage us the same way. It also encourages us to be wise, to be gracious, and to carefully answer every person who asks us about our lifestyle.

STEWARDSHIP PRINCIPLE: Christ is Lord over all. Every part of our life should reflect our faithful stewardship to him. Our families, our children, our friends, our employees, our colleagues should be able to see the stewardship of God in our lives daily.

1 Thessalonians

Being faithful stewards will produce holiness. Becoming Obedient Owners is not an easy task. Someone once said being successful in life is 10% inspiration and 90% perspiration. The Apostle practiced this during his life and ministry.

Paul reminds them that he worked among them as a missionary pastor

Becoming Obedient Owners is not an easy task.

without thinking of himself as anything but a humble servant.

Never once did we try to win you with flattery, as you well know. And God is our witness that we were not pretending to be your friends just to get your money! (1 Thess. 2:5 NLT)

It was not about money but about ministry.

But we don't need to write to you about the importance of loving each other, for God himself has taught you to love one another. Indeed, you already show your love for all the believers throughout Macedonia. Even so, dear brothers and sisters, we urge you to love them even more. Make it your goal to live a quiet life, minding your own business and working with your hands, just as we instructed you before. Then people who are not Christians will respect the way you live, and you will not need to depend on others. (1 Thess. 4:9-12 NLT)

STEWARDSHIP PRINCIPLE: Work hard as a steward. Be mission driven. Be ready to go to heaven at any time. It is not about the money, but rather about ministry. Love one another. Mind your own business and don't depend on others to meet your needs; depend upon God.

2 Thessalonians

The theme of this second letter to the church at Thessalonica is similar to the first letter: Be ready for the return of the Lord in his second coming. A steward is a hard worker, not a lazy, unproductive member of society. He earns a living, cares for his family, and pays his own way.

And now, dear brothers and sisters, we give you this command in the name of our Lord Jesus Christ: Stay away from all believers who live idle lives and don't follow the tradition they received from us. For you know that you ought to imitate us. We were not idle when we were with you. We never accepted food from anyone without paying for it. We worked hard day and night so we would not be a burden to any of you. We certainly had the right to ask you to feed us, but we wanted to give you an example to follow. Even while we were with you, we gave you this command: "Those unwilling to work will not get to eat." Yet we hear that some of you are living idle lives, refusing to work and meddling in other people's business. We command such people and urge them in the name of the Lord Jesus Christ to settle down and work to earn their own living. (2 Thess. 3:6-12 NLT)

Stewards honor God by working hard and encouraging those around them to work hard as well.

STEWARDSHIP PRINCIPLE: Honor God with your labors. Welcome hard work and the opportunity to help yourself with the fruits of your labor. Encourage others to practice obedient ownership by working hard as well.

1 Timothy

Paul hung out in Ephesus for at least three years and discipled a young house church pastor named Timothy. He admonished these new believers to allow the gospel to change their lives. They needed to be different from those around them. He even shared with them a stewardship message: they should look at money and possessions in a godly way.

Now there is great gain in godliness with contentment, for we brought nothing into the world, and we cannot take anything out of the world. But if we have food and clothing, with these we will be content. But those who desire to be rich fall into temptation, into a snare, into many senseless and harmful desires that plunge people into ruin and destruction. For the love of money is a root of all kinds of evils. It is through this craving that some have wandered away from the faith and pierced themselves with many pangs. (1 Tim. 6:6-10 ESV)

In 6:17-19, Paul gave three commands to Timothy and those house church members regarding stewardship.
1. Command them to be holy because he is holy!
2. To be rich in good deeds implement the Great Commission and the Great Commandment. Reach the lost and love your neighbor.

Use money for God's glory.

3. Be willing to share financially. Be a generous and systematic donor.

How is this for a job description for a true biblical steward?

STEWARDSHIP PRINCIPLE: Use money for God's glory. Don't love it and allow it to rule your life. As a steward, be godly in your lifestyle, practice good deeds, and give generously.

2 Timothy

Paul encourages his young coworker to fight the good fight of faith and persevere in spite of suffering. The journey of the steward is not always an easy path. There will be trials and tribulations along the way. He invites this young house pastor to be faithful and pass along the message of being a faithful steward and soldier.

> *... be strong through the grace that God gives you in Christ Jesus. You have heard me teach things that have been confirmed by many reliable witnesses. Now teach these truths to other trustworthy people who will be able to pass them on to others. Endure suffering along with me, as a good soldier of Christ Jesus. Soldiers don't get tied up in the affairs of civilian life, for then they cannot please the officer who enlisted them. And athletes cannot win the prize unless they follow the rules.* (2 Tim. 2:1-5 NLT)

Paul also admonishes Timothy to preach the Word, the gospel, the stewardship principals, and the whole council of God. "Work at telling others the Good News, and fully carry out the ministry God has given you." (2 Tim. 4:5 NLT). It is a strong command.

STEWARDSHIP PRINCIPLE: Be a steward and pass that message, tradition, practice, and passion along to others. As an Obedient Owner you will fulfill your mission and calling in life.

Titus

Paul wrote this book to one of his traveling companions, a first-century church leader named Titus. It is a book based upon principles of stewardship, the link between faith and practice and belief and behavior. Titus was a church leader and Paul admonished all church and lay leaders.

I have been sent to proclaim faith to those God has chosen and to teach them to know the truth that shows them how to live godly lives. (Titus 1:1b NLT)

Paul indicated some basic expectations for an elder and steward. He should be:

well thought of ... committed to his wife ... looked up to ... not pushy, not short-tempered, not a drunk, not a bully, not money hungry ... he must welcome people, be helpful, wise, fair, reverent, have a good grip on himself [can I hear someone say "stewardship"], *and on the Message ... knowing how to use the truth to either spur people on in knowledge or stop them in their tracks if they oppose it.* (Titus 1:6-9 THE MESSAGE)

Those are all indicators of a wise and generous New Testament steward.

STEWARDSHIP PRINCIPLE: A faithful steward is one whose faith and belief match up with their practice and behavior.

Philemon

This book is about the power of the gospel to change lives and friendships. First Paul praises his friend Philemon for his generosity then asks his wealthy friend for a favor.

I am praying that you will put into action the generosity that comes from your faith as you understand and experience all the good things we have in Christ. (Philemon 1:6 NLT)

Then Paul asked for a pass for his new convert, a former slave of Philemon's named Onesimus. Paul asked his friend Philemon to receive his former slave just as he would receive Paul.

So if you consider me your partner, welcome him as you would welcome me. If he has wronged you in any way or owes you anything, charge it to me. (Philemon 1:17-18 NLT)

You would only have a conversation like this with a close friend. This is not an exchange between two strangers.

STEWARDSHIP PRINCIPLE: Thank your friends and those faithful stewards around you and challenge them to do even more with their resources to further the gospel.

Hebrews

Faith is a key factor in the life of the steward. This book speaks of Christ's superiority over all and the need for us to endure and to be faithful in all things. It evens defines faith as "the confidence that what we hope for will actually happen; it gives us assurance about things we cannot see." (Heb. 11:1 NLT)

Faith is a better way of life. Stewardship is a better way of life. Twenty-five times in the book the words "better," "more," and "greater" appear. The comparative seems to be that Christ is

Faith is a key factor in the life of the steward.

greater and better than the law of the Old Testament. It follows, then, that a New Testament lifestyle-giving concept is better than the levitical tax (the tithe of the Old Testament).

The discipline of sacrificing all we have and are to God and to his work is a biblical stewardship concept.

Keep on loving each other as brothers and sisters. Don't forget to show hospitality to strangers, for some who have done this have entertained angels without realizing it! Remember those in prison, as if you were there yourself. Remember also those being mistreated, as if you felt their pain in your own bodies. Don't love money; be satisfied with what you have. For God has said, "I will never fail you, I will never abandon you." So we can say with confidence, "The LORD is my helper, so I will have no fear. What can mere people do to me?" (Heb 13:1-3, 5-6 NLT)

STEWARDSHIP PRINCIPLE: Display your stewardship by being an Obedient Owner, faithful, hospitable, kind, and loving. Be grateful for what you have and acknowledge its source.

James

We are encouraged, even admonished, to be a "doer" and not just a "hearer" of the word. This entire book is one devoted to stewardship principles. Here are a few of the themes that roll out of the key verse 2:17: "So also faith by itself, if it does not have works, is dead" (ESV).

1. Ask for wisdom (1:5)
2. The wealthy should be humble (1:10)
3. Every gift in life is from God (1:17)
4. Be doers of the word, not just hearers (1:22)
5. Do not show partiality (2:1ff)
6. Show mercy (2:13)
7. Show your faith by your works (2:18)
8. Control your tongue (chapter 3)
9. Resist the devil, draw near to God (4:7-8)
10. Our plans are destined to fail without God (4:13-15)
11. Rich folks beware (5:1-6)
12. Confess your sins and pray for one another (5:13-19)

The practical lifestyle guidelines of a biblical steward are here in these five chapters. Read the book of James once a month until it becomes your lifestyle.

STEWARDHIP PRINCIPLE: You will find no less than 12 principles from the book of James alone to consider and apply to your life. Any or all of them will help you become a more Obedient Owner.

1 Peter

This book shares with its readers how to live out a life of faith and stewardship in both good and the bad times. We do that through obedience even when persecution comes our way.

You yourselves like living stones are being built up as a spiritual house, to be a holy priesthood, to offer spiritual sacrifices acceptable to God through Jesus Christ. (1 Peter 2:5 ESV)

A spiritual sacrifice you can offer to the Lord is to live your life as a true biblical steward, "having purified your souls by your obedience to the truth." (1 Peter 1:22 ESV)

Peter shares another stewardship moment.

Most important of all, continue to show deep love for each other, for love covers a multitude of sins. Cheerfully share your home with those who need a meal or a place to stay. God has given each of you gifts from his great variety of spiritual gifts. Use them well to serve one another. (1 Peter 4:8-10 NLT)

Have you ever seen a check written from the "Bank of Heaven?" Nor have I. God doesn't have a checkbook. He owns it all. We have checkbooks, and we are those "living stones" who can invest our time, talent, and treasure generously so God's generosity can flow though us.

Ever seen a check written on the Bank of Heaven?

STEWARDSHIP PRINCIPLE: In good and bad times, practice stewardship through love, hospitality, and generous sharing of your financial resources.

2 Peter

Is it easy to make the sacrifice of a steward when those around us do not? This book teaches that the grace of God in Christ truly transforms and empowers Christians to live the life of a steward even in the face of opposition. This book concludes in chapter 3 with a reminder about preparation. We need to be ready at any time to give an account of our time here on this earth because "the day of the Lord will come as unexpectedly as a thief" (2 Peter 3:10a NLT).

We have all been guilty of the sin of procrastination. I will be a good giver when I have more money. I will invest time in my church or favorite ministry when the kids are gone away to college. I will lend my expertise and talent to God and his business when it's not so stressful at my business.

Our churches and Christian organizations are full of three classes of stewards and workers. "Shirkers" are always able to wiggle out of any agreement to serve. "Jerkers" always sign up and start out with a lot of passion and energy, but after jerking out of the starting blocks they quickly fade away. "Workers" do the heavy lifting in most church and parachurch organizations. They show up and are there from start to finish. They invest their time, their talent, and of course their treasure in preparation for the return of the Lord.

STEWARDSHIP PRINCIPLE: Stewardship starts now, not at a time when it's convenient. Be prepared, because there will be a heavenly audit of our investments here on earth.

1 John

John the Beloved calls his readers to reconsider these three basics of the life of a steward: true doctrine, obedient ownership (there it is again), and fervent devotion. He speaks of God as the "Light of the World" and his Son Jesus Christ as the manifestation of that light. He speaks of joy—reminding me that some of the happiest, most joyful people I have ever met are biblical stewards.

I want to confess my sin of having been a poor steward at times. At times I have misused resources God entrusted to me to manage for his glory, and have been a disobedient owner. Money and possessions can be strong temptations to be untruthful and untrustworthy. That temptation can lead to sin. I am comforted in John's writings, where he says,

> *If we claim we have no sin, we are only fooling ourselves and not living in the truth. But if we confess our sins to him, he is faithful and just to forgive us our sins and to cleanse us from all wickedness. If we claim we have not sinned, we are calling God a liar and showing that his word has no place in our hearts.* (1 John 1:8-10 NLT)

I can be forgiven for my thoughtless decisions as a steward, and I know God will not reject me for my past bad behavior.

Perhaps his strongest message of stewardship is in chapter 2.

Do not love this world nor the things it offers you, for when you love the world, you do not have the love of the Father in you. For the world offers only a craving for physical pleasure, a craving for everything we see, and pride in our achievements and possessions. These are not from the Father, but are from this world. And this world is fading away, along with everything that people crave. But anyone who does what pleases God will live forever. (1 John 2:15-17 NLT)

STEWARDSHIP PRINCIPLE: If you are obedient and fervent in your stewardship walk and allow the light of God's Word to shine on your investments of work, wisdom, and wealth, you will be blessed eternally and live with God forever.

2 John

This short epistle is about the two key factors in any relationship. If love and truth are evident, most relationships have a great opportunity to be successful. Stewards must be motivated to love God with all of their being and always be truthful. Are you being honest with your investments in God's kingdom? We are either living the life of an Obedient Owner or we are being influenced by the world and being deceived or led astray.

How happy I was to meet some of your children and find them living according to the truth, just as the Father commanded. I am writing to remind you, dear friends, that we should love one another. This is not a new commandment, but one we have had from the beginning. Love means doing what God has commanded us. (2 John 1:4-6a NLT)

STEWARDSHIP PRINCIPLE: Apply love and truth to all stewardship decisions and you will not be deceived but will walk in the light of Christ.

3 John

Here we go again with those issues of love and truth. John has encouraged a believer in one of his church plants (a man named Gaius) to be steadfast in his faith and to live as a steward in the face of opposition.

This appears to be the only place in scripture where the term "good health" is used.

The elder to the beloved Gaius, whom I love in truth. Beloved, I pray that all may go well with you and that you may be in good health, as it goes well with your soul. For I rejoiced greatly when the brothers came and testified to your truth, as indeed you are walking in the truth. I have no greater joy than to hear that my children are walking in the truth. (3 John 1:1-4 ESV)

I believe it is impossible to walk in the truth and light of God's Word without being a steward. Can I ask you to give some thought to verse 2 where the soul and good health are used in the same sentence? I will not propose that generous stewards are healthier than those who are not. You make the call. What did John mean by using both of those words in the same sentence?

STEWARDSHIP PRINCIPLE: Love people, not things, and walk in God's truth. Your life and health will be impacted by your obedient ownership.

Jude

Jude presents an expanded version of truth and encourages the saints to contend for the true faith that has been delivered to us through the revelation that is God's Word. The way to practice that true faith is to resist false teaching and diligently follow the truth which includes becoming a biblical steward.

His opening remarks have a stewardship connotation.

To those who are called, beloved in God the Father and kept for Jesus Christ: May mercy, peace, and love be multiplied to you. (Jude 1:1-2 ESV)

We are called as stewards to practice mercy, peace, and love in all our doings.

Jude then spends the next thirteen verses of this very short book encouraging first century Christians to watch out for false teachers, ungodly people, and those who would pervert the truth of God. He even mentions the delivery of Israel from Egypt and those angels who fell with Lucifer. Our stewardship battle is not just against flesh and blood but against powers of darkness.

Is this a description of Madison Avenue—encouraging mindless spending and overextension of our ability to pay by slick advertising and greedy methodology?

But you must remember, beloved, the predictions of the apostles of our Lord Jesus Christ. They said to you, "In the last time there will be scoffers, following their own ungodly passions." It is these who cause divisions, worldly people, devoid of the Spirit. (Jude 1:17-19 ESV)

STEWARDSHIP PRINCIPLE: Practice God's principles of stewardship and not the world's version of materialism. The world is presenting its package that follows its own ungodly passions.

Revelation

A true biblical steward is in almost constant conflict as the world's system calls them to think about themselves and not others. Unbelievers and non-practicing stewards often use their work, their wisdom, and their wealth to further their own causes and desires, not the work of God. John's book, written while he was in exile, unveils the spiritual war in which the church is engaged—the cosmic conflict between the triune God on the one hand and Satan and his evil allies (both demonic and human) on the other.

Jesus won the ultimate battle on the cross, but his church continues to be assaulted through persecution, false teaching, and the allure of material affluence and cultural approval. The world says spend your money, waste your time, and misuse your God-given

A biblical steward is in constant conflict with the world's system.

talent. We were created to bring honor and glory to God our Father, yet many have lost their way in this great conflict.

The book of Revelation is the culmination of all stewardship principles. Through praise and worship, the glory of God may be seen in creation, revelation, incarnation, and resurrection. God created this world, and for thousands of years since the fall, the Prince of the Power of the Air (Satan) had influence on this world; but that will all come to an end when Satan and his angels are tossed into a bottomless pit, there to suffer eternal damnation.

Then the seventh angel blew his trumpet, and there were loud voices shouting in heaven: "The world has now become the Kingdom of our Lord and of his Christ, and he will reign forever and ever." (Rev. 11:15 NLT)

God will then have his world back just as he had it in Genesis 1:1, where he created the heavens and the earth. The beginning and the end will have come together again. God will be totally in charge with Satan in total retreat.

God will honor your labors and mine to be a true steward.

STEWARDSHIP PRINCIPLE: We are reminded that the Alpha and Omega owns it all and that we have been assigned to be good stewards for this season until Christ returns to redeem it all.

Conclusion

All thirty-nine books of the Old Testament and all twenty-seven books of the New Testament contain stewardship themes, concepts, and principles. Perhaps I am winning you over to see the Word of God is not only a book of redemption, but also one of stewardship.[26] I want to remind you again that it is my goal to move the "obedient ownership" concept into our Christian vocabulary. Our goal as believers must be to manage according to the will of God the Father, who is the ultimate owner of all things.

---

[26] Many of the New Testament themes used in this chapter were from the new ESV study Bible published in 2008 by Crossway Bibles. It is one of the best study Bibles available.

11
Bankruptcy

"Many a man has failed because he had his wishbone where his backbone should have been." — Ronald Reagan

"If your vision is for a year, plant wheat. If your vision is for ten years, plant trees. If your vision is for a lifetime, plant people." — Chinese Proverb

"Keep your eyes on your destination ... and not where you stumbled." — Nigerian Proverb

Within the Internal Revenue Service there are a number of types of bankruptcy filings. The two most widely know are Chapter 7 and Chapter 11. When a business is unable to service its debt or pay its creditors, the business or its creditors can file with a federal bankruptcy court for protection under either filing. In Chapter 7 the business ceases operations; a trustee sells all of its assets and then distributes the proceeds to its creditors. Any residual amount is returned to the owners of the company.

For Chapter 11, in most instances the debtor business remains in control of its business operations as a debtor in procession, and is subject to the oversight and jurisdiction of the court. More specifically, Chapter 11 permits reorganization under the bankruptcy laws, as opposed to liquidation. In most cases the reorganization period lasts 120 days. It is available to every business, whether organized as a corporation or sole proprietorship, and to individuals, although it is most prominently used by corporate entities. Executor contracts may be canceled under Chapter 11 if it is in the best interest of the business, and like other bankruptcy forms, creditors are prevented from taking any action against the debtor and cannot demand collection of debts owed.

Based upon these textbook definitions, I believe we may be on the verge of declaring a state of bankruptcy here in America and the Western World. I am no doomsday prophet; in fact, at times I have been accused of being a "criminal optimist." I always try to see the best. We live in a great nation. However I think the 3 P's of Haggai's culture—the Priests, the Princes, and the People—are also here in our nation, and have experienced a form of spiritual, cultural, financial, and political bankruptcy. We seem to be experiencing many of the same conundrums they encountered.

Here are the issues Haggai addressed with the bankrupt nation of Israel/Judah.

Consider Your Ways: The Theme Of Haggai

1. Living in luxurious houses while the temple—the Jewish national symbol—lies in ruin

182

2. Despite planting lots of crops, there is little or no harvest
3. Food is plentiful but no one gets filled up; people are hungry
4. Wine is plentiful but everyone is thirsty
5. They have clothing to wear but not sufficient to stay warm
6. Wages are fair, but lost because of holes in the pockets and bad investments
7. No one seems to want to hear what God or his prophet have to say about our lifestyle choices
8. They consider their own way the best way, figuring they can solve their own dilemma

For America and the world, some additional items could be added to Haggai's list.

1. A failed banking system
2. An economic meltdown unprecedented since the 1930's
3. Rampant corporate fraud
4. Troubling bankruptcy filings by large and prominent international corporations
5. Consumer credit card debt at an all time high
6. Foreclosure rates that are the highest in our nation's history
7. Unemployment rates at historic highs (in the state of Michigan, near 20%)
8. Widespread uncertainty regarding the future
9. Fear for jobs (77% of Americans polled)
10. The stock market and wealth losses at an all time high
11. Other international banking systems in chaos (i.e. UK leaders apologize to the nation for losing their money)[27]

And this list is by no means exhaustive. All you have to do is pick up your local newspaper or read your Internet news source. If you look in the business, money, or investment section, the news is often rather gloomy. Words and phrases like these are often viewed, "The Worst in our History," "Chaos," "The Plan is not working," "Debt is crippling our nation," "The largest national deficit in our nation's history."

Are you discouraged? Are you frightened? Are you anxious? I think we're ready for answers to this economic downturn. We're ready to learn about an eternal stimulus package. I assure you it's a simple plan, but it is counterintuitive to our culture.

Embezzlement

We are on the edge of fiscal, spiritual, cultural, and political bankruptcy for one simple yet profound reason. We are embezzlers! We have stolen from God.

How can the God of this universe become a victim of a crime? Are any of us big enough to mug God and steal from him? Can we pull out a gun and threaten the Alpha and the Omega? Can any of us hack into the Bank of Heaven computer system and relieve The Great I Am of a few thousand or million of dollars? The answer to all of these scenarios is a flat out "NO!"

> *We are on the edge of fiscal, spiritual, cultural, and political bankruptcy.*

Yet Malachi 3:8 asks the question, "Why do you rob God?" Clearly we do, and we do it by embezzling what belongs to him.

As Christians, are our giving patterns or our spending patterns our first consideration? Remember, the theme of this book is "obedient ownership." When we take what is not ours we become embezzlers.

If you take advantage of your employer or help yourself from your little league baseball fund or from your elderly parent or grandparent, it's stealing. It's clearly a form of robbery or the minor prophet would not have mentioned it. The tax system of the Old Testament and the lifestyle-giving admonitions of the New Testament are ignored by many who attend church and claim to be followers of Christ. Managing your resources according to the will of the owner, God the Father, is no easy task.

Crime of Intent

To make sure I was not missing out on the real intent of embezzlement I asked some people on both sides of the issue for their opinion. I asked a former judge and a practicing attorney to wade in on these issues and give you some real practical down-home experiences. These interviews were with people who have tried and defended embezzlers and who have presided over court cases involving embezzlement.

The Honorable Justice Henry Deneen, Esq., now a ministry CEO, told me he always sentenced an embezzler to the maximum allowed by the law because he considered embezzlement a "crime of intent," not a "crime of passion." Crimes of passion involve a moment or two of very bad judgment in the heat of the moment. Not so with the embezzler. He or she broke the law over a long period of time. It was a crime of the heart.

The human heart is the most deceitful of all things, and desperately wicked. Who really knows how bad it is? (Jer. 17:9 NLT)

Kevin Knowlton is a partner in the law firm Peterson and Meyers in Florida. He described the embezzler as a person who converts assets or monies owned by someone else to their own personal ill-gotten gain. Attorney Knowlton felt most embezzlers intended to pay back the money they stole, but it gets out of hand. He shared that it is very difficult to defend the embezzler. No matter how sophisticated they have become, there is usually an incriminating paper or electronic trail. The evidence usually ends up fortifying the prosecutor's case. He also agreed that embezzlement is crime of intent, a crime of the heart that often unfolds over many months and years.

> *Embezzlement is a crime of intent.*

Very few people are feeling sorry for the Bernie Madoffs of this world. He took money from investors and friends in an intricate ponzi scheme that significantly increased his own personal wealth. He was a sophisticated embezzler, apparently driven by greed. Much like our narrative from Haggai describes, his life and his heart were defiled and everything he touched was also defiled.

Society or Scripture

Only one of these is going to win out as we look at the whole issue of stewardship. Which will have the greater impact—the society in which we live or the Word of God—on how we live our lives, how we invest, how we spend and give? Are we going to obey God and seek to become a biblical steward, or are we going to listen to the siren call of society? "Toys R Us" is a great store unless frequenting it becomes our lifestyle. Adult toys are expensive too. One of the ways we make sure we can fund our lifestyle is to embezzle our tithes and offerings.

Do we think the Bible really means what it says about stewardship and how we manage our resources?

I am talking about the practice of stewardship that transcends Wall Street, recessions, and depressions; it transcends the ups and downs of our economy. Are you willing to be a steward when your 401K is in the tank? Do you have faith in God's Word and your stewardship plan that transcends government regulations and politics? When

Toys-R-Us is a bad lifestyle for adults.

push comes to shove, who is it that you choose to honor? We don't need another survey to read the Word and hear its clear message **to become generous** and compassionate. See that you "grow in the grace of giving" was theme the apostle Paul presented and enhanced with the believers in Corinth.

Keeping Up with the Joneses

Most of us understand peer pressure, even if it's implicit. If our neighbor puts in a pool, we feel we need a pool as well. If our neighbor gets a new car, we get the itch to trade in the "clunker" for a sleek new model. But we are not trying just to keep up with our neighbors anymore; that's old school. No way! We want to far exceed the Joneses. They put in a three-lap pool, and we feel the need for one with six lanes. They build a 5,000 square foot home, and we need one with 7,500 square feet.

Bigger is not always better. More "bling" does not always mean more blessings—usually just the opposite. When we reach this point, we don't own and manage our stuff; it owns us. We have become disobedient owners.

Even with all the space we have (homes are much bigger today than they were twenty years ago) we still don't have enough room for all of our stuff. The self-storage industry fact sheet indicates 1 out of every 10 Americans currently rents a storage unit. There are 52,753 self-storage companies in the USA. Help me out here; is there something wrong with this picture? We feel the need to not only have as much stuff as the Joneses, but a whole lot more stuff than the Joneses.

Do we need a 12-step AA type program for us ownership junkies? The meeting would go something like this, "Hello, my name is Pat and I love and worship my stuff. I am an ownership junkie." Or perhaps, "Hello, my name is Pat and in my effort to keep up with the Joneses I rent two large storage units because I don't have room for all my stuff at home, in the attic, in my garage or in the shed out back. I am an ownership junkie."

Is there an AA type of program for ownership junkies?

The Three Most Important Things in Life to Manage

I expect some pushback for that subtitle, but being a graduate of a Baptist seminary it's difficult to get over that three-point sermon. We have mentioned our time, talent, and treasure many times; I know you have that down by now. Another way to look at all of this is from an investment perspective. To any life experience I bring my work (time), my wisdom (talent), and my wealth (treasure).

Please allow me to give you another very simple way to look at becoming a biblical steward. If I can bring these three distinct parts of my life under God's authority, I am on the way toward true stewardship.

ME (Who I Am)

The core values of my being must be submitted to God, the ultimate steward. By becoming a disciple and growing into an Obedient Owner, my life begins to make a difference—not just over the next ten years, but even in the next ten minutes.

Begin that first step to purpose in your heart to commit your life to follow God wholeheartedly so you can have your own ME statement. Need a commitment verse or two? There are lots of them. Here are a couple of my favorites.

The Pharisees and Sadducees were trying once again to trip up Jesus and gather additional charges for his upcoming trial. They asked him a question from the law: "What is the greatest commandment?" He gave them an interesting answer, not just one commandment, but two.

Jesus replied, "'You must love the Lord your God with all your heart, all your soul, and all your mind.' This is the first and greatest commandment. A second is equally important: 'Love your neighbor as yourself.' The entire law and all the demands of the prophets are based on these two commandments." (Matt. 22:37-40 NLT)

That needs to be ME. What if my personal mission statement was reflective of those two commandments—to love God with a whole heart and to love my neighbor.

A friend many years ago challenged me to imagine sitting at my own wake and hearing people up front talk about Patrick McLaughlin. What would I want said about ME?

I did hear an amusing version of an epitaph recently. It went like this:

Here lies the bones of Mary Jones
whose life it had no tares.
She lived as an old maid, she died as an old maid.
No runs, no hits, no errors.

None of us wants that eulogy. We need to be mission driven in our lives and our investment of ME, in the world where God has placed us to serve.

STEWARD'S STEP: Write a personal mission statement and begin to think through your own eulogy, what you want said in your final service. What part of that mission statement do you have at work right now in your life's work and ministry? None of us hits a home run every time, but we can hit some singles and doubles and a triple or two.

My Thing (What I Do)

The ME part of all this was who you are. Now comes MY THING—what I do for a living and how I can make my work a ministry. As we grow into Obedient Owners, our God-given talent is something we need to invest in kingdom work. I don't believe there is work that is secular and work that is sacred; there is no dichotomy. Stewardship is everything we do after we say we believe. Hence from that point forward we are 24-7 stewardship servants, investing our time, our talent and treasure in ensuring that God's work moves forward.

If we are mission-driven then everything we do is the mission and ministry of our life. If God calls me to be a plumber or a builder or a stockbroker or a teacher or a pastor, it's all the same. I need to let my light shine before men so they can see my good works and glorify God. Honesty, integrity, hard work, loving and caring for my coworkers and my customers are important parts of MY THING.

My thing!

My mother used to quote this statement as she raised us: "If a task is once begun, never leave it until it's done; be the labor great or small, do it well or not at all." If I am working at Starbucks for peanuts or in a Manhattan bank for big bucks, I need to serve Jesus in that position. Yes, your work and my work matter to God. He is concerned with MY THING.

My Things (What I Have to Obediently Own)

This is the hardest of the three to own and manage wisely. It is so easy to become proud or possessive of our things. "I have more than my neighbor, God must somehow love me more than him!" That is just not the case. We all have lots of stuff, in most cases too much stuff. Once again we must be careful to love people and use things in an obedient way rather than using people and loving our things! An asset screening will tell you what a person has, but it does not tell you anything about their heart. There are lots of people who live in gated communities who don't really have big money, but they do in fact have big mortgages. This whole housing industry collapse that's still going on (just like in Haggai) is an issue of greed and the desire for more things, bigger things, bigger houses, more bling, you know exactly what I am talking about. Nearly every one of us knows someone who believed the lie and let their passion for things they could not afford impact their present and future financial situation.

My things!

Generosity is not related to our things or our net worth. Some very wealthy Christians are paupers when it comes to investing their time, their talent, and their treasure in God's work. They are managing their things according to their own plan, not God's plan. Frankly, they are "disobedient owners." Regardless of our lot in life or the value of our things, we all need to be "rich in faith" as mentioned in James 2:5. It does not matter where we live, the make and model of the car we drive, or how much gold and silver is in our account, the issue with our

Generosity is not related to our net worth.

things is once again "Obedient Ownership," managing according to the will of the Owner.

It's A Wrap

We cannot hoard our time; as we all know, time marches on. We cannot hoard our talent; we must use it or lose it. But we can and do hoard our treasure. All three of these are critical components to honoring God as "Obedient Owners." God brought an entire nation to its knees economically, and a prophet named Haggai helped them once again become rich in faith and trust the Owner. We can look back to 500 BC and learn some valuable lessons. If we are not obedient, at some point God is going to address our disobedience. Ask yourself these questions:

- Have I planted much, but harvested very little?
- Do I eat, but just never seem to have enough to satisfy?
- Am I always thirsty even though I have plenty to drink?
- Do I have nice warm clothes, but always seem to be underdressed and cold?
- Do I make good or at least decent money, but put it into a wallet with holes in it?

These are the questions Haggai asked the Children of Israel in the first chapter of his prophetic book. Remember, five times Haggai challenged them to "give careful thought to their ways."

If stewardship/obedient ownership was not important why did those who penned the inspired Word of God all mention it in their 66 canonized books? There are more stewardship references than any other theme in the Bible. Here's why! God our Father, the Owner, knew how much trouble we would have living our lives as "Obedient Owners." Hey it's tough! But it's something we must strive to do to grow in our faith. I believe obedience and blessings may have common threads. Sure, I know there are very poor people who are rich in faith, but whether I have a little or a lot, I need to manage it in an obedient way.

If stewardship is truly everything we do after we say we believe, then our only goal is obedience. All parts of my life must be managed according to the will of the Owner so I will one day enter His presence and hear these words, "well done thou faithful servant" you have proven yourself as an "Obedient Owner."

---

[27] *London Times,* Fall 2009.

Bible Study Questions from the book of Haggai

1. What segments of society were addressed by the prophet Haggai?

   _____

   _____

   _____

   _____

   _____

2. Why the hold up on rebuilding the temple?

   _____

   _____

   _____

   _____

   _____

3. How did God get their attention? Does God still work this way?

_____

_____

_____

_____

4. Is there a better way to say, "Give Careful Thought to Your Ways"? (today's language)

_____

_____

_____

_____

5. Does God still work the same way today as He did in Haggai 1:9-11?

_____

_____

_____

6. There are two key words/phrases in verses 12 & 13 – how are they related?
   • Obedience _____
   • I am with you _____

_____

_____

7. How much time elapsed between verse 1 and verse 13?

_____

_____

_____

8. How much time elapsed between Chapter 1:1 and Chapter 2:1?

   _____

   _____

9. Give a modern day translation of Haggai 2:3-9. What did the former temple look like—does "be strong and work" speak about us today? What are those words of comfort once again mentioned? Why the big shake up in vs. 6-7? What about the present temple of worship as contrasted with the former?

   _____

   _____

   _____

   _____

   _____

   _____

   _____

   _____

   _____

   _____

   _____

   _____

   _____

   _____

   _____

   _____

10. Read verses 10-14, what is defiled in our culture today?

_____

_____

11. Define the significance for the Children of Israel and us in verses 15-19.

_____

_____

_____

_____

_____

_____

_____

12. What is the promise God makes to them and us in verse 20ff and what is a modern day signet ring? Is God really proud of them and proud of us sometimes?

_____

_____

_____

_____

13. The bottom line of Haggai written around 520 BC is Obedient/Ownership. Is this the same bottom line today 2,500 years later?

_____

_____

_____

_____

14. Share a practical use of Haggai in your own life as a person called to "Disciple Stewards."

_____

_____

_____

_____

_____

_____

15. Last question—Why aren't these 38 verses preached more in our churches?

_____

_____

_____

_____

_____

_____

_____

_____

_____

_____

_____

_____

_____

_____

_____

Stewardship Quiz

1. What a man does with his money is between him and God only *(no other human involvement)*.
   T or F

2. Is it OK to personally ask people in our churches to invest their resources in the ministry?

Y or N	Talent	*Will you sing in the church choir?*
Y or N	Time	*Will you teach a Bible class?*
Y or N	Treasure	*Will you give generously $3,000 - $5,000 to help accomplish a specific church ministry need?*

3. One third of Jesus' earthly ministry revolved around the teaching of stewardship, the investment of time, talent, and treasure.
   T or F

4. The New Testament does not emphasize the <u>tithe</u>, but does emphasize "life style giving."
   T or F

5. Who conducted the first capital campaign recorded in the scriptures?
   ❏ Abraham
   ❏ Moses
   ❏ Joshua

6. Who personally asked a gentile (unsaved) king for his participation in an Old Testament capital project?
   ❏ Nehemiah
   ❏ Isaiah
   ❏ Hosea

7. Micah clearly stated "You will not be blessed because you have robbed God." *(trick question)*
   T or F

8. a) The apostle Paul believed in pledges and secured a commitment from which New Testament church:
   ❏ Ephesus
   ❏ Corinth
   ❏ Phillipi
   b) Who was the gift solicited for? _____

9. Paul instructed Timothy to ask the house church in Ephesus for money, just for the purpose of demonstrating their faith.
   T or F

10. Paul told the Corinthians that "God loves a cheerful giver," but he will take it from a grouch. I Corinthians 16
    T or F

11. Ananius and Sapphira died because they did not give enough money to God and to the church in the book of Acts.
    T or F